Cambridge Proficiency
Examination Practice 4

Cambridge Proficiency

Examination Practice 4

University of Cambridge
Local Examinations Syndicate

CAMBRIDGE
UNIVERSITY PRESS

PUBLISHED BY THE PRESS SYNDICATE OF THE UNIVERSITY OF CAMBRIDGE
The Pitt Building, Trumpington Street, Cambridge, United Kingdom

CAMBRIDGE UNIVERSITY PRESS
The Edinburgh Building, Cambrige CB2 2RU, UK   http://www.cup.cam.ac.uk
40 West 20th Street, New York, NY 10011–4211, USA   http://www.cup.org
10 Stamford Road, Oakleigh, Melbourne 3166, Australia
Ruiz de Alarcón 13, 28014 Madrid, Spain

First published 1991
Seventh printing 1999

Printed in the United Kingdom at the University Press, Cambridge

A catalogue record for this book is available from the British Library

ISBN 0 521 40730 3 Student's Book
ISBN 0 521 40731 1 Teacher's Book
ISBN 0 521 40729 X Set of 2 Cassettes

Contents

To the student

This book is for candidates preparing for the University of Cambridge Certificate of Proficiency in English examination and provides practice in all the written and oral papers. It contains 5 complete tests, based on the Proficiency examinations set in 1988 and 1989, and incorporates the modifications made to Paper 5 (the Interview) in December 1987. The examination consists of 5 papers, as follows:

Paper 1 Reading Comprehension (1 hour)
Section A consists of 25 multiple-choice items in the form of a sentence with a blank to be filled by 1 of 4 words or phrases.
Section B consists of 15 multiple-choice items based on 2 or more reading passages of different types.

Paper 2 Composition (2 hours)
There are 5 topics from which you choose 2. The topics include discursive, descriptive and narrative essays, a directed writing exercise and an essay based on optional reading. (In these practice tests the questions based on optional reading are set on the kind of books that are prescribed each year. These are *not* the actual books prescribed for any particular year: they are just given as examples.)

Paper 3 Use of English (2 hours)
Section A contains exercises of various kinds which test your control of English usage and grammatical structure.
Section B consists of a passage followed by questions which test your comprehension and skill in summarising.

Paper 4 Listening Comprehension (about 30 minutes)
You answer a variety of questions on 3 or 4 recorded passages from English broadcasts, interviews, announcements, phone messages and conversations. Each passage is heard twice.

Paper 5 Interview (15 to 20 minutes)
You take part in a conversation based on a photograph, passage and other material from authentic sources linked by theme, either with a group of other candidates or with the examiner alone. The exercises in these tests include some of the type set in the examination on optional reading.

Practice Test 1

PAPER 1   READING COMPREHENSION   (1 hour)

Answer all questions. Indicate your choice of answer in every case **on the separate answer sheet** *already given out, which should show your name and examination index number. Follow carefully the instructions about how to record your answers. Give* **one answer only** *to each question. Marks will not be deducted for wrong answers: your total score on this test will be the number of correct answers you give.*

SECTION A

In this section you must choose the word or phrase which best completes each sentence. **On your answer sheet** *indicate the letter A, B, C or D against the number of each item 1 to 25 for the word or phrase you choose.*

1   Religion and politics interest him almost ....
    A equally   B the same   C similarly   D alike

2   Our salesmen normally .... their travel expenses from the company once a month.
    A settle   B reimburse   C cover   D claim

3   A property company was making a take-over .... for the supermarket site.
    A proposition   B bid   C tender   D proposal

4   .... had they recovered from the first earthquake when they felt the second tremor.
    A Never   B Scarcely   C No sooner   D Just

5   These suggestions are .... to be accepted by the majority of members.
    A unlikely   B impossible   C undoubtedly   D inconceivable

6   The train .... the bay and then turned inland for twenty miles.
    A coasted   B skirted   C edged   D sided

7   I'm not keen on .... control of the project to a relative newcomer.
    A undertaking   B charging   C entrusting   D allotting

8   Our party chairman is .... great admirer of the Prime Minister.
    A some   B very   C no   D not

9   I'm afraid we haven't got a spare bed. Can you .... with a mattress on the floor?
    A make do   B make by   C make over   D make up

10 .... receipt of your instructions, I immediately sent a telex message to Algeria.
    A On   B In   C With   D By

11 I'm sure that never happened – it's just a .... of your imagination.
    A fantasy   B figment   C piece   D picture

12 He was unable to keep up the pace .... by the first three runners.
    A set   B staged   C created   D led

13 At first the children enjoyed the game but quite soon the novelty ....
    A went off   B died out   C died down   D wore off

14 The desk was so .... with papers that it was hard to find anything.
    A burdened   B cluttered   C overrun   D muddled

15 I have several problems at the moment, ... the least of which is lack of money.
    A but   B not   C only   D far

16 He phoned to tell me that he couldn't come tomorrow because he .... to the dentist.
    A had gone   B was going   C would go   D went

17 The increase from 5 million to 350 million speakers of English has not .... because of any special merits in the language itself.
    A come to   B come up   C come about   D come forward

18 There has been a great deal of .... in the press about the results of the murder trial.
    A speculation   B prediction   C contemplation   D sensation

19 To make the sauce, ... a small bar of chocolate and melt it over a pan of water.
    A splash   B hack   C grate   D cut

20 The new Garden City is well worth .... if you're in the area.
    A being seen   B a visit   C to visit   D the sight

21 What .... the smoke and the noise, the party made me feel quite ill.
    A because of   B through   C owing to   D with

22 The illness spread .... all our attempts at keeping it in check.
    A regardless   B contrary   C despite   D against

23 Many road accidents occur because motorists cannot .... the speed of approaching vehicles.
    A assume   B count   C assess   D value

24 It's hard to believe that anyone would purposely harm a child, ... of all its own mother.
    A first   B least   C worst   D best

25 You've been overworking recently, and would find a holiday ....
    A benevolent   B essential   C beneficial   D profitable

SECTION B

In this section you will find after each of the passages a number of questions or unfinished statements about the passage, each with four suggested answers or ways of finishing. You must choose the one which you think fits best according to the passage. **On your answer sheet**, *indicate the letter A, B, C or D against the number of each item 26 to 40 for the answer you choose. Give* **one answer only** *to each question. Read each passage right through before choosing your answers.*

FIRST PASSAGE

As I was putting this book on Computer Assisted Language Learning (CALL) together, I could almost hear the collective groan rising up from staff and common rooms throughout the land: surely not *another* breezy little introduction to the mighty micro, *more* pressure on us to dabble in expensive, irrelevant and time-consuming technology at a time when the teacher is struggling simply to survive in an increasingly harsh world. Most teachers are hard put to find the price of a box of chalk, let alone of a roomful of microcomputers.

Such a reaction is, to put it mildly, easy to comprehend, particularly at a time of much general political tub-thumping about the need to embrace the chip or perish, to espouse what is vaguely dubbed "information technology", without the well-meaning generalities having yet been satisfactorily translated into positive action on the ground (with a few laudable exceptions). Computers are now supposed to be operating across the curriculum, but one microcomputer to a thousand pupils is not likely to achieve this end for a very long time. Hence it is not to be wondered at that the school of criticism which cheerfully asserted "I have not read such-and-such a book but I think it should be banned" is alive and well among the anti-computer lobbyists.

There is no escaping the fact that CALL is new and, like all new things, treated by one camp with deep suspicion, and by a handful of enthusiasts with over-optimistic glee. It has been condemned on the one hand as impersonal and educationally unsound, and praised to the skies on the other as ushering in a new era of open, interactive and creative learning. As usual the truth lies somewhere in between, and it is my purpose to determine precisely where the truth is to be located.

This book does not set out to present, from the cushioned comfort of my academic ivory tower, an enthusiastic hymn of praise to the micro, which seeks to lay down the law as to how this new technological miracle must be used by the hard-pressed teacher to resolve all his problems. What follows is based on practical experience of CALL, not only at university level, but with teachers' groups and a research project investigating the feasibility and desirability of extending the role of the computer in modern language teaching in schools.

26 What sort of response to his book does the writer expect from teachers?
   A   amused
   B   hostile
   C   frightened
   D   cautious

27 According to the writer, many politicians believe that
   A   computers are expensive and irrelevant.
   B   it is dangerous to rely on computers.
   C   a knowledge of computers is essential.
   D   only a few pupils will benefit from computers.

28 The writer claims that the attitude of the 'anti-computer lobbyists' is
   A   understandable.
   B   astonishing.
   C   distressing.
   D   contemptible.

29 What is the author's stated aim in writing the book?
   A   to examine the past use of CALL in schools
   B   to encourage students to make use of CALL
   C   to strengthen interest in CALL among teachers
   D   to weigh up the advantages and disadvantages of CALL

30 To which expected criticism from teachers does the writer reply in the last paragraph?
   A   He is uncritical of CALL.
   B   CALL is more suitable for university students.
   C   The research done on CALL is inadequate.
   D   His knowledge of CALL is too theoretical.

SECOND PASSAGE

As Morgan watched, he saw Fanshawe and his wife go up and chat to Adekunle, who smiled and beamed at them with urbane geniality. He saw Fanshawe, in response to some remark of Adekunle's, laugh uneasily and shoot a quick glance over his shoulder up at the first-floor windows. Morgan swiftly pulled himself back behind the wall though he was fairly sure he couldn't be seen. Typical Fanshawe, he fumed inwardly, the man clearly wasn't suited for this undercover work if he revealed the position of his confederates so thoughtlessly. It was time, he decided, that he went down and sorted things out.

As he slowly descended the stairs on his way to meet Adekunle, he felt his pulse quicken and a tight ball of pressure establish itself securely in his stomach. He stepped out of the back entrance of the Commission and onto the crowded lawn.

As he weaved his way through the groups of people towards Adekunle, he could feel his palms moistening and his mouth drying. Adekunle was a large man. He was going steadily to fat as all successful Kinjanjans seemed inevitably to do – as if it were a natural outcome of power and esteem – and he had about him an aura of unshakeable self-confidence. He was talking seriously and in a low voice to his wife, who looked sullen beneath her headdress and who was smoking a cigarette, nervously staring down at the trampled grass. As Morgan drew near they both looked up, smiling suddenly in a well-practised insincere way.

"Professor Adekunle," Morgan said, "how do you do? I'm Morgan Leafy, First Secretary here at the Commission. I think we met once briefly before." This was not true, they had only been in the same room, but it was his favourite introductory device, often throwing people into confusion as they racked their brains trying to remember the occasion. It had no such effect on Adekunle. He smiled beneath his wide moustache.

"Did we? I'm afraid I don't recall, but how do you do anyway." He shook Morgan's hand. "This is my wife, Celia."

"Hello," Celia Adekunle said in a demure voice. She kept her eyes on Morgan's face. As with all direct looks that he received, he found this one somewhat disconcerting; he suspected they stirred vast untapped reservoirs of guilt deep within him. He returned to Adekunle.

31 What is Morgan doing at the beginning of the passage?
    A   talking to Fanshawe and his wife
    B   talking to Adekunle
    C   hiding in the garden
  ✓D   keeping out of sight upstairs

32 What is the relationship between Morgan and Fanshawe?
    A   They have never met before.
    B   They are both friends of Adekunle.
    C   They are working together.
    D   They dislike one another.

33 What do the smiles of Adekunle and Celia suggest?
    A   They are pleased to see Morgan.
    B   They are used to appearing in public.
    C   They have been quarrelling with each other.
    D   They feel apologetic about the damaged lawn.

34 Adekunle's reaction to Morgan's first remark is
    A   a disappointment to Morgan.
    B   embarrassing to everyone present.
    C   exactly what Morgan expected.
    D   satisfactory in the circumstances.

35 Which of the people mentioned in the passage never shows any nervousness?
    A   Morgan
    B   Celia
    C   Adekunle
    D   Fanshawe

THIRD PASSAGE

There can be few who would knowingly condone waste, whether of energy, of manpower or of financial assets. So why does our educational system make so little provision for those who, given the opportunity, could best help society achieve its objectives and expand its horizons?

Support programmes have long been established for children with learning difficulties and under-achievers. People argue that the resources are inadequate to meet the existing need and that greater efforts must be made, but at least the problem is being faced.

At the opposite end of the ability scale is a group of children which one would logically expect to offer the greatest challenge and yield the greatest rewards, both for the children themselves and for society as a whole. Sadly, special provisions in this area are few and far between.

Regional and district child guidance departments are all too conscious of the fact that some 2 per cent of the school population falls within the "gifted" category. Many have ready prepared lists of children in their areas who have high ability, in the hope of a positive programme of action being initiated at national or regional level. Lack of funds cannot be held wholly responsible for the seeming indifference to the problem.

People think a "gifted" child has enough good fortune to be gifted and needs no further help. But such children are not always the happy and fulfilled young people one might expect. Classmates' derision, mental boredom and frustration are not easy to live with, at best creating apathy and resignation, at worst invoking a rebellious response in the form of anti-social behaviour.

Potential ability does not blossom without help and encouragement. All great artists and musicians have needed to be taught the techniques of their craft and to explore the work of others, before embarking on their own creations. It has been said that a masterpiece is made up of 10 per cent genius and 90 per cent hard work. The power of concentration of these children and their capacity for work is extremely high and their thirst for wider experience apparently insatiable. With judicious handling they can produce amazing results in a short period of time.

It is said that many children of high intelligence do not allow themselves to be "discovered" – for fear of becoming an outcast. Rather than risk losing their friends because of their high ability, they often conceal their potential talents.

36 The author suggests that our education system
    A   spends money extravagantly.
    B   encourages children to expand their horizons.
    C   spends enough money on unusual children.
    D   neglects the needs of gifted children.

37 According to the author, children with learning difficulties
    A   are given more help than gifted children.
    B   have too much money spent on them.
    C   must face up to their problems.
    D   deserve more support than other children.

38 Child guidance departments in some areas
    A   are already helping gifted children.
    B   are aware of the needs of gifted children.
    C   have a high proportion of gifted children.
    D   want gifted children to be dealt with by central government.

39 If gifted children are unhappy, they may
    A   reject further help.
    B   turn against their friends.
    C   start to misbehave.
    D   refuse to attend school.

40 What is needed to bring out the best in gifted children?
    A   a peaceful environment
    B   stimulating teaching
    C   a knowledge of art and music
    D   strict discipline

PAPER 2   COMPOSITION   (2 hours)

*Write **two only** of the following composition exercises. Your answers must follow
exactly the instructions given. Write in pen, not pencil. You are allowed to make
alterations, but see that your work is clear and easy to read.*

1   Describe those aspects of your life that give you the greatest pleasure.
    (About 350 words)

2   "The economic benefits of nuclear power outweigh the potential dangers."
    Discuss this statement. (About 350 words)

3   Write a story which ends as follows: "The telephone stopped ringing.
    Briefcase in hand, Evelyn went out slamming the door." (About 350 words)

4   You are a journalist. Printed below are 4 short news telexes. Choose **two
    only**, and for each one you choose, write a newspaper article of about 150
    words.

A.   U.N. TEAM CLIMBS EVEREST. PARTY OF 5 SCALES PEAK AFTER
     6 DAYS OF APPALLING TRAGEDY. ORIGINAL TEAM OF 10 CUT
     DOWN BY ILLNESS, ACCIDENTS AND MYSTERIOUS
     DISAPPEARANCES. TEAM LEADER VOWS NEVER TO CLIMB AGAIN.

B.   LIFE IN OUTER SPACE DECLARES U.S. NOBEL PRIZE WINNING
     SCIENTIST. SPACE CREATURES PAY ME REGULAR VISITS,
     TAKE ME ON TRIPS IN UFOS. WORLD WILL EXPLODE IN YEAR
     2000, THEY CLAIM. SPACE COLONIES THE ONLY WAY TO
     PREVENT EXTERMINATION OF OUR SPECIES.

C.   GOLD DISCOVERED IN CENTRAL LONDON. MINING ENGINEERS
     FIND MASSIVE DEPOSITS OF ORE UNDER WESTMINSTER ABBEY.
     GOVERNMENT DENY PLANS TO DEMOLISH ABBEY, BUT REFUSE
     TO CONFIRM EXISTENCE OF EXPLORATORY SHAFT.

D.   UNITED MOTOR COMPANY LAUNCHES NEW FAMILY CAR. 4 WHEEL
     DRIVE. 6 GEARS. BUILT-IN COMPUTER NAVIGATES AND
     CONTROLS FUEL CONSUMPTION. AUTOMATIC DISTRESS BEACON
     FOR EASY LOCATION BY EMERGENCY SERVICES IN CASE OF
     ACCIDENT. AVAILABLE WORLDWIDE BY END NEXT MONTH.
     HATCHBACK AND SALOON VERSIONS, BLACK OR RED ONLY.
     STEREO EXTRA.

5   Basing your answer on your reading of the prescribed text concerned,
    answer **one** of the following. (About 350 words)

D.H. LAWRENCE: *Selected Tales*
What impressions do these stories give of family life in a small community?

JOHN OSBORNE: *The Entertainer*
What difference is there between Archie Rice on stage and Archie Rice at
home?

ANITA BROOKNER: *Hotel du Lac*
What part do the letters to David play in the novel?

PAPER 3   USE OF ENGLISH   (2 hours)

SECTION A

1   *Fill each of the numbered blanks in the following passage with* **one** *suitable word.*

It is widely recognised that we must automate our industry or else we shall find .... (1) unable to compete. But technical changes in the field of automation are .... (2) rapid that it is difficult for anyone not directly involved to understand .... (3) and what they imply. One cannot reasonably expect the .... (4) Member of Parliament, mainly concerned .... (5) he is bound to be with the many day-to-day problems of .... (6) constituency, to go much more deeply .... (7) the subject than to examine the likely .... (8) of automation upon employment, and therefore .... (9) voting, in his area. Yet, fortunately, politics are not only the .... (10) of politicians, but necessarily involve the .... (11) of citizens. .... (12) is an urgent political task to educate the people as a .... (13) so as to make them .... (14) of the broad problems and opportunities of automation, and we must strive .... (15) a national policy .... (16) this issue. One of the bases on which .... (17) a policy ought to rest is an organisation, perhaps .... (18) up jointly of government, industry and trade unions, which .... (19) engage in a vigorous drive to .... (20) people understand the full implications of automation.

2   *Finish each of the following sentences in such a way that it is as similar as possible in meaning to the sentence printed before it.*

EXAMPLE: His second attempt on the world record was successful.

ANSWER: He broke *the world record at his second attempt.*

a)   We couldn't have managed without my father's money.
     If it *hadn't been for my father's money we wouldn't have managed*

b)   I had only just put the phone down when the boss rang back.
     Hardly *had I put the phone down my boss rang back*

c)   It was Walter Raleigh who introduced potatoes and tobacco into England.
     The English owe *it to Walter Raleigh for the introduction of potatoes and tobacco*

d)   "If my members agree to that I'll be very surprised," said the union delegate.
     The union delegate observed that *he will be very surprised if his members reached an agreement.*

e)   While I strongly disapprove of your behaviour, I will help you this time.
     Despite my *disapprovement of your behaviour I still am willing to help you this time*

f)   I'm sorry I missed Professor Baker's lecture.
     I'm sorry not *being able to attend Professor baker's lecture*

g)   We may not be able to give the concert.
     The concert *might not happen.*

h)   I was not surprised to hear that Harry had failed his driving test.
     It came *as no surprise that harry had failed his driving test*

3   *Fill each of the blanks with a suitable word or phrase.*

EXAMPLE: He doesn't mind one way or the other; it makes *no difference to* him.

a)   It .... Helen who borrowed the record player, could it?

b)   He prefers driving .... driven.

c)   It's about .... finished that report.

d)   Don't marry him! You'd .... living by yourself.

e)   "I'm sorry to keep you waiting."
     "Not at all. It .... least."

f)   If I had known you weren't coming I .... to such trouble.

4   *For each of the sentences below, write a new sentence* **as similar as possible in meaning to the original sentence**, *but using the word given. This word* **must not be altered** *in any way.*

     EXAMPLE: Not many people attended the meeting.
              turnout

     ANSWER: *There was a poor turnout for the meeting.*

a)   We'd better leave them a note, because it's possible they'll arrive later.
     case

     ....

b)   Before he came here he worked for Mr Smith.
     previous

     ....

c)   He speaks German extremely well.
     command

     ....

d)   His criticisms are quite unfair.
     justification

     ....

e)   I can't understand why they are reluctant to sign the contract.
     baffled

     ....

f)   I always find chess problems like that quite impossible!
     defeat

     ....

g)   This must be kept secret.
     know

     ....

⟫→

13

h) I can't afford a new dress; that old blue one will have to do.
    make

....

SECTION B

5   *Read the following passage, then answer the questions which follow it.*

People don't like getting their hands dirty. Rubbish disposal has always been left to society's lower ranks, with an "out of sight, out of mind" attitude from people not directly involved. Today, however, both the increase in the amount and the complexity of waste produced are threatening human health and the environment as never before. The   5
composition of waste has altered, the most dramatic change being in the number of chemicals we dump. Chemicals in the form of pills, pesticide or paint are an essential part of our lives. The disposal of waste from this chemical feast has amplified existing shortcomings in the way we treat rubbish, forcing us to confront what we would rather throw away.   10
Contamination of water, air and soil is widespread. Lead in the air affects our brains. Heavy metals in the soil are taken up by plants and passed on to us when we eat them. The environment takes a toll as well. Trees are dying from acid rain. Rivers run black with pollution. Mysterious green waste from petro-chemical factories mar fields where   15
children play.

The increase in complexity of waste has caught disposal authorities on the hop and today's hazardous waste is showing up the cracks in the disposal systems. The most common form of waste disposal is the "tip", nowadays called a landfill. Landfills are holes in the ground in which   20
rubbish is deposited. The rubbish settles and then decomposes. Liquids seep through into the earth and down into the groundwater, into the water which we drink and use. Nature can cope with a little such abuse but the quantity and toxicity of waste have outstripped Nature's restorative powers. In order to cope with the problem of containing toxic   25
oozings, modern landfill sites are lined with impermeable plastic or clay which can isolate their contents. But this is still a short-term measure: landfills will eventually leak.

Some rubbish is disposed of by incineration. The effectiveness of this depends on what you are burning, at what temperature and where the   30
smoke-borne waste finally lands. Black smoke means that whatever is in the incinerator is not burning thoroughly. This can increase the danger to the environment, as in the case with certain chemicals found in lubricants, electrical transformers and a host of other things that we use every day. These chemicals are among the most poisonous ever pro-   35
duced, and are very difficult to get rid of. High-temperature incineration is thought to destroy them, but if they are burned at a lower temper-

14

ature, deadly toxins are emitted. High-temperature incineration, however, requires expert handling and specialised kilns, so it is expensive.

Dumping waste straight into the sea is especially popular with island   40
nations such as Britain. The UK treats the seas around it as a personal
dustbin, emptying most of its sewage there and allowing industries to
jettison their effluvia into the fishy depths. Britain's dumping of nuclear
waste in the Atlantic has caused a storm of outrage and the practice has
halted for the time being. But overtures are being made to other   45
countries to pave the way for dumping waste in their territorial waters,
far away from the vocal voters at home with their "not in my backyard"
attitude to waste.

Another way of dealing with waste is to recycle it. Industry is
beginning to see the benefits in reclaiming its toxic cast-offs. Nothing,   50
however, can beat prevention and we all have our parts to play. We only
have to look in our dustbins. Bleaches, fluorescent light tubes, paint
thinners, nail polish, fly sprays and garden chemicals all add to the toxic
problems. Households don't produce as much waste as industry, yet it
can be just as deadly.   55

a)   What is an "out of sight, out of mind' attitude? (line 2)

....

....

b)   Explain why human health and the environment are more at risk than
ever before.

....

....

c)   How has the disposal of chemical waste "amplified existing shortcomings in the way we treat rubbish"? (lines 9–10)

....

....

....

》》》→

d) Explain the phrase "to confront what we would rather throw away". (line 10)

    ....

    ....

e) What word or phrase could be used in place of "on the hop"? (lines 17–18)

    ....

f) What is meant by "showing up the cracks"? (line 18)

    ....

    ....

g) What is the "abuse" referred to in line 23?

    ....

    ....

h) What attempts are made to stop contamination of the groundwater?

    ....

    ....

    ....

i) Explain the phrase "a short-term measure". (line 27)

    ....

j) Why does black smoke indicate added danger to the environment?

    ....

    ....

k) Explain the phrase "jettison their effluvia into the fishy depths". (line 43)

....

....

l) Why are "overtures being made to other countries to pave the way for dumping waste in their territorial waters"? (lines 45–46)

....

....

m) What is meant by "to recycle it"? (line 49)

....

....

n) What does the word "prevention" (line 51) refer to?

....

....

o) In a paragraph of 70–90 words, state the methods of dealing with waste and their advantages and disadvantages as described by the author of the passage.

....

....

....

....

....

....

....

PAPER 4   LISTENING COMPREHENSION
(about 30 minutes)

PART ONE
You will hear a lecturer in a college talking about British history. For each of the questions 1–4, tick one of the boxes A, B, C or D to show the correct answer.

1   Which lecture in the series is this?

A   first

B   third

C   fourth

D   fifth

A	
B	
C	
D	

2   How long is each lecture?

A   5 minutes

B   15 minutes

C   50 minutes

D   55 minutes

A	
B	
C	
D	

3   This series of lectures covers British history up to

A   the time of Julius Caesar.

B   410 AD.

C   the time of Henry VIII.

D   the present.

A	
B	
C	
D	

4   Why does the lecturer pause after saying "... a long period in British history"?

A   He wants to close the door.

B   He loses his notes.

C   There is a lot of noise.

D   Someone comes in late.

A	
B	
C	
D	

PART TWO
You will hear a discussion on the radio about cable television. For each of the questions 5–12, tick one of the boxes to show whether the statement is true or false.

	True	False
5 Cable TV allows more channels to be broadcast.		
6 More people can watch cable TV.		
7 TV reception is improved with cable TV.		
8 Cable TV companies will be able to transmit anything there is a market for.		
9 It offers better pictures at a higher price.		
10 It is agreed that cable TV will improve programme content.		
11 The British are likely to use American technology.		
12 British Cable will probably convey more than 100 channels.		

PART THREE
You will hear an interview with the author of a new cookery book. For each of the questions 13–15, tick one of the boxes A, B, C or D to show the best answer.

13 She says that the main difference between herbs and spices in cooking is that

A herbs enhance the flavour more than spices.	A
B the use of too much spice can spoil the food.	B
C spices are necessary for cooking, but herbs are not.	C
D spices have to be used in combination with oils and essences.	D

19

14 Why does she advise against using commercially-prepared curry powder?

   A It ruins the flavour of the food.

   B There is too great a variety to choose from.

   C It contains whole spices.

   D It has no distinctive flavour.

A	
B	
C	
D	

15 What does she say about her recipes?

   A She has suggested using a lot of spice in them.

   B They do not need to be followed strictly.

   C She recommends steaming curries.

   D They are the result of a lot of experiment.

A	
B	
C	
D	

PART FOUR

You will hear Mr Anstey being asked some questions about the proposed conversion of Littlebury Hall into a Technical Training Centre. For questions 16–24, fill in the survey sheet with short answers or by ticking one of the boxes A, B, C or D.

PROPOSED CONVERSION OF LITTLEBURY HALL TO TECHNICAL TRAINING CENTRE

SURVEY SHEET

PERSONAL DETAILS:

NAME ___16___

AGE ___17___

OCCUPATION ___18___

RESIDENT SINCE ___19___

20 ANTICIPATED DISRUPTION DURING BUILDING WORKS:

A INTOLERABLE ☐

B SEVERE ☐

C SLIGHT ☐

D NONE ☐

21 PRESENT SHOPPING AMENITIES WILL BE:

A PERFECTLY ADEQUATE ☐

B JUST ADEQUATE ☐

C NOT ADEQUATE ☐

D TOTALLY INADEQUATE ☐

22 CHARACTER OF AREA WILL BE:

A THE SAME AS NOW ☐

B IMPROVED ☐

C CHANGED FOR THE WORSE ☐

D UTTERLY RUINED ☐

23 RENTED ACCOMMODATION IN THE VICINITY:

A NONE ☐

B LIMITED, BUT CHEAP ☐

C PROBABLY SUFFICIENT ☐

D TOO EXPENSIVE FOR STUDENTS ☐

24 TRAFFIC PROBLEMS ARISING FROM DEVELOPMENT:

A NEGLIGIBLE ☐

B INSURMOUNTABLE ☐

C MANAGEABLE WITH CAREFUL PLANNING ☐

D NONE FORESEEN ☐

PAPER 5 INTERVIEW (15–20 minutes)

You will be asked to take part in a conversation with a group of other students or with your teacher. The conversation will be based on one particular topic area or theme, for example holidays, work, food.

Of course each interview will be different for each student or group of students, but a *typical* interview is described below.

* At the start of the interview you will be asked to talk about one of the photographs among the Interview Exercises at the back of the book.

* You will then be asked to discuss one of the passages at the back of the book. Your teacher may ask you to talk about its content, where you think it comes from, who the author or speaker is, whether you agree or disagree with it, and so on. You will *not* be asked to read the passage aloud, but you may quote parts of it to make your point.

* You may then be asked to discuss for example an advertisement, a leaflet, extract from a newspaper etc. Your teacher will tell you which of the Interview Exercises to look at.

* You may also be asked to take part in an activity with a group of other students or your teacher. Your teacher will tell you which section among the Interview Exercises you should look at.

Practice Test 2

PAPER 1   READING COMPREHENSION   (1 hour)

*Answer all questions. Indicate your choice of answer in every case **on the separate** **answer sheet** already given out, which should show your name and examination index number. Follow carefully the instructions about how to record your answers. Give **one answer only** to each question. Marks will not be deducted for wrong answers: your total score on this test will be the number of correct answers you give.*

SECTION A

*In this section you must choose the word or phrase which best completes each sentence. **On your answer sheet** indicate the letter A, B, C or D against the number of each item 1 to 25 for the word or phrase you choose.*

1   Employees who have a .... are encouraged to discuss it with the management.
   A hindrance   B disturbance   C disadvantage   D grievance

2   This travel guide is very useful, but it does not .... to cover every aspect of the country.
   A claim   B announce   C state   D expect

3   It's the Prime Minister's right to .... an election at any time he likes.
   A summon   B nominate   C call   D submit

4   .... his advice, I would never have got the job.
   A Except   B Apart from   C But for   D As for

5   The unscrupulous salesman .... the old couple out of their life savings.
   A deprived   B swindled   C robbed   D extracted

6   I heard the sound of the blind man .... with his stick.
   A creaking   B ticking   C pattering   D tapping

7   I can't write that kind of letter unless I'm in the right .... of mind.
   A frame   B way   C set   D turn

8   The Health Minister was .... in a private hospital last week.
   A operated   B admitted   C cared   D treated

9 Can you .... the BBC World Service on your new radio?
   A put on   B take in   C get at   D pick up

10 Speed limits on the road .... to protect pedestrians as well as motorists.
    A serve   B prove   C succeed   D intend

11 Tax .... deprives the state of several million pounds a year.
    A retention   B desertion   C escapism   D evasion

12 A few political extremists .... the crowd to attack the police.
    A animated   B agitated   C incited   D stirred

13 Mr Jones wants twenty copies of this letter .... off on the photocopier.
    A put   B run   C taken   D turned

14 What you say is true, but you could have .... it more tactfully.
    A talked   B phrased   C observed   D remarked

15 For the experiments to succeed, the measurements must be accurate to
    .... five centimetres.
    A about   B under   C within   D exactly

16 The situation was .... complicated by John's indecision.
    A more   B extra   C further   D altogether

17 A few hours after the injection the feeling of numbness in your arm will
    ....
    A wear off   B fade out   C drop away   D fall through

18 It's no .... waiting for a bus: they don't run on public holidays.
    A good   B point   C worth   D reason

19 I could see the tip of his cigarette .... in the darkness.
    A glowing   B sparkling   C gleaming   D glinting

20 A managing director cannot expect to have much time to .... to purely
    personal matters.
    A reserve   B devote   C concentrate   D spare

21 If you .... in behaving in this way you will bring yourself nothing but
    trouble.
    A persist   B continue   C decide   D react

22 Fred says that his present job does not provide him with enough ....
    for his organising ability.
    A scope   B space   C capacity   D range

23 Many local authorities realise there is a need to make .... for disabled
    people in their housing programmes.
    A assistance   B conditions   C admittance   D provision

24 I'd like to .... this old car for a new model but I can't afford it.
    A interchange   B exchange   C replace   D convert

25 He spent his entire life .... round the world, never settling down
    anywhere.
    A scattering   B scrambling   C transporting   D roaming

SECTION B

*In this section you will find after each of the passages a number of questions or
unfinished statements about the passage, each with four suggested answers or ways of
finishing. You must choose the one which you think fits best according to the passage.*
On your answer sheet, *indicate the letter A, B, C or D against the number of each
item 26 to 40 for the answer you choose. Give* **one answer only** *to each question.
Read each passage right through before choosing your answers.*

FIRST PASSAGE

Diversity is a hallmark of life, an intrinsic feature of living systems in the
natural world. The demonstration and celebration of this diversity is an endless
rite. Look at the popularity of museums, zoos, aquariums and botanic gardens.
The odder the exhibit, the more different it is from the most common and
familiar life forms around us, the more successful it is likely to be. Nature does
not tire of providing oddities for people who look for them. Biologists have
already formally classified 1.7 million species. As many as 30 to 40 million more
may remain to be classified.

Most people seem to take diversity for granted. If they think about it at all
they assume it exists in endless supply. Nevertheless, diversity is endangered
as never before in its history. Advocates of perpetual economic growth treat
living species as expendable. As a result, an extinction crisis of unprecedented
magnitude is under way. Worse yet, when diversity needs help most, it is
neglected and misunderstood by much of the scientific community that once
championed it.

Of the two great challenges to the legitimacy of this diversity, the familiar one
comes primarily from economists. Their argument, associated with such names
as Julian Simon, Malcolm McPherson and the late Herman Kahn, can be
paraphrased: "First, if endangered species have a value as resources – which
has been greatly exaggerated – then we should be able to quantify that value so
that we can make unbiased, objective decisions about which species, if any, we
should bother to save, and how much the effort is worth. Secondly, the global

25

threat to the diversity of species, particularly in the tropics, has been overestimated. Thirdly, we have good substitutes for the species and ecosystems that are being lost, and these substitutes will nullify the damage caused by the extinctions".

The structure of the argument seems to me to be identical in form to that of an old joke from the American vaudeville circuit. One elderly lady complained to another about her recent vacation at a resort in the Catskill Mountains in New York State. "The food was terrible", she moaned. "Pure poison. I couldn't eat a bite. And the portions were so tiny!"

Species may be valuable, but not especially so, and the threat to them has been exaggerated. But this does not matter anyway, say the economists, because we can replace any species that vanishes.

It is not clear how much of an impact this argument has on the informed public, but it has certainly provoked an outcry among scientific conservationists. It has set the terms for, and dominated, most of the pro-diversity literature of the past few years, making it a literature of response, thus limiting its scope and creative force.

26 Which feature of the natural world do people find especially fascinating?
    A   its great variety
    B   its ancient forms
    C   its strange rituals
    D   its unclassified species

27 Which adjective best describes the writer's attitude towards the scientific community?
    A   respectful
    B   supportive
    C   critical
    D   uncomprehending

28 Which statement represents the views of economists?
    A   It is important to conserve endangered species.
    B   Endangered species have no value in themselves.
    C   Only some parts of the natural world are under threat.
    D   New species could be introduced as necessary.

29 What point is the writer trying to make about the economists' arguments by including the joke in paragraph 4?
    A   Their case is overstated.
    B   Their logic is unsound.
    C   They are unduly pessimistic.
    D   They ignore the views of ordinary people.

30 Of which paragraph is paragraph 5 a summary?
   A Paragraph 1
   B Paragraph 2
   C Paragraph 3
   D Paragraph 4

31 The position of the scientific conservationists has been weakened because
   they have
   A adopted the economists' arguments.
   B failed to communicate with the public.
   C lost the initiative in the debate.
   D protested too loudly.

SECOND PASSAGE

We threaded our way out of the noise and confusion of the Customs shed into
the brilliant sunshine on the quay. Around us the town rose steeply, tiers of
multi-coloured houses piled haphazardly, green shutters folded back from their
windows, like the wings of a thousand moths. Behind us lay the bay, smooth as
a plate, smouldering with that unbelievable blue.

Larry walked swiftly, with head thrown back and an expression of such regal
disdain on his face that one did not notice his diminutive size, keeping a wary
eye on the porters who struggled with his trunks. Behind him strolled Leslie,
short, stocky, with an air of quiet belligerence, and then Margo, trailing yards of
muslin and scent. Mother, looking like a tiny, harassed missionary in an
uprising, was dragged unwillingly to the nearest lamp-post by an exuberant
Roger, and was forced to stand there, staring into space, while he relieved
pent-up feelings that had accumulated in his kennel. Larry chose two magnifi-
cently dilapidated horse-drawn cabs, had the luggage installed in one, and
seated himself in the second. Then he looked round irritably.

"Well?" he asked. "What are we waiting for?"

"We're waiting for Mother," explained Leslie. "Roger's found a lamp-post."

"Dear God!" said Larry, and then hoisted himself upright in the cab and
bellowed, "Come on, Mother, come on. Can't the dog wait?"

"Coming, dear," called Mother passively and untruthfully, for Roger showed
no signs of quitting the post.

"That dog's been a damned nuisance all the way," said Larry.

"Don't be so impatient," said Margo indignantly; "the dog can't help it . . .
and anyway, we had to wait an hour in Naples for you."

"My stomach was out of order," explained Larry coldly.

"Well, presumably his stomach's out of order," said Margo triumphantly.

At this moment Mother arrived, slightly dishevelled, and we had to turn our
attentions to the task of getting Roger into the cab. He had never been in such a
vehicle, and treated it with suspicion. Eventually we had to lift him bodily and
hurl him inside, yelping frantically, and then pile in breathlessly after him and

hold him down. The horse, frightened by this activity, broke into a shambling trot, and we ended in a tangled heap on the floor of the cab with Roger moaning loudly underneath us.

"What an entry," said Larry bitterly. "I had hoped to give an impression of gracious majesty, and this is what happens . . . we arrive in town like a troupe of medieval tumblers."

32 What does the town appear to be like?
  A   untidy
  B   flat
  C   picturesque
  D   modern

33 What did Mother's behaviour suggest?
  A   She was deliberately wasting time.
  B   She was angry with Larry.
  C   She preferred the dog to her children.
  D   She couldn't control the situation.

34 What made the dog panic?
  A   the noise on the quay
  B   Larry's shouting
  C   the horse-drawn cab
  D   the heat of the day

35 Larry was disappointed at the end of the passage because
  A   the cabs were in poor condition.
  B   the family were so slow.
  C   their arrival looked ridiculous.
  D   Margo kept arguing.

36 The overall impression of Larry is that he was
  A   tolerant.
  B   self-important.
  C   undignified.
  D   unintelligent.

THIRD PASSAGE

In New York, hype is hope. It is not so much a dishonest or a cynical activity as a naive expression of faith in a future whose potential is always more attractive than the actuality of the present. Television news shows and chat shows, for example, rely on trailers of future items in order to keep their audience. Trailers promise an excitement and a potential which are always yet to be fulfilled and therefore yet to disappoint; they divert attention away from the material actually being broadcast, because such material always fails to live up to the claims made for it. The reality of television news shows is so much the opposite of the potential they wish to embody that their only role is to be constantly disposed of or abandoned. Where British television flatters all its programmes by the courtesy of polite continuity, television in New York is a fragmented succession of interruptions, abbreviations, and abrupt edits. The outcome is a product which fails to satisfy because it lacks respectful treatment, and it lacks respectful treatment because it fails to satisfy.

The same applies to New York's buildings. Behind the plush facades and marble foyers which serve as come-ons to the prospective shopper or business client or hotel guest, the sophistication breaks down. Those parts of the building meant to be out of bounds to the public, or which only get visited by service staff – fire escapes, service corridors, rear entrances, and delivery points – are often quite remarkably crude. Not just unadorned, but so horribly cheap in their construction, in the clumsy threading of essential cables and plumbing, in the unintended uses they are put to (notably, temporary storage), and their general state of upkeep, that it is amazing that they go on working, that the supply of mains water still reaches the topmost floors, or that the worn electric wiring does not short across the metal down-pipes.

This is the reality that lies behind the facade, made possible by its relationship with the facade. To lure more shoppers and clients and guests, New York buildings do what television does, and proclaim on their exteriors the coming attractions of their interiors. To do this they pinch pennies from the utilitarian parts of the building, since these represent reality and reality is, if not expendable, then at least too mundane to be worth consideration. This automatically rules out the possibility of all parts of a building being treated with equal care.

37   The writer claims the people in New York
    A   expect the future to surpass the present.
    B   dream about the future because of their present poverty.
    C   make promises about the future that they do not intend to keep.
    D   have lost faith in the present.

38 Television news programmes in New York maintain their audience by
    A   showing fast-paced programmes.
    B   giving previews of coming attractions.
    C   concentrating on interesting stories.
    D   presenting diverting interviews.

39 The respect that British television has for its programmes is shown by its
    A   lack of fragmentation.
    B   greater sophistication.
    C   self-satisfaction.
    D   more courteous presenters.

40 The writer complains that New York's buildings are
    A   badly designed.
    B   cheaply constructed.
    C   uncared for in some areas.
    D   clumsily decorated throughout.

PAPER 2   COMPOSITION   (2 hours)

*Write **two only** of the following composition exercises. Your answers must follow exactly the instructions given. Write in pen, not pencil. You are allowed to make alterations, but see that your work is clear and easy to read.*

1   Describe someone who has greatly influenced your life and explore the reasons for this influence. (About 350 words)

2   "A sense of humour is the most important of all human qualities." Do you agree? (About 350 words)

3   "As the train began to pull out of the station, they dashed on to the platform and hurled themselves into a compartment." Use this as the first or last sentence of a short story. (About 350 words)

4   You have recently received a number of comments from local residents, some of which are printed below. As representative of the local committee of residents, write a letter to the authorities outlining people's concerns and suggesting what should be done. (About 300 words)

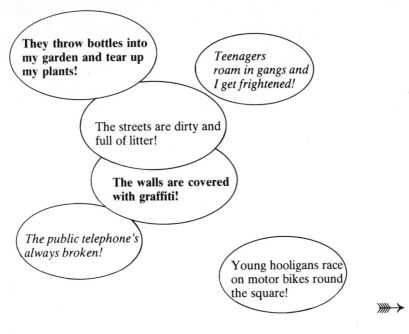

They throw bottles into my garden and tear up my plants!

Teenagers roam in gangs and I get frightened!

The streets are dirty and full of litter!

The walls are covered with graffiti!

The public telephone's always broken!

Young hooligans race on motor bikes round the square!

⟫→

5 Basing your answer on your reading of the prescribed text concerned, answer **one** of the following. (About 350 words)

GRAHAM GREENE: *The Quiet American*
Fowler said of Pyle: "I never knew a man who had better motives for all the trouble he causes". Discuss this statement commenting on the motives and the trouble.

JANE AUSTEN: *Persuasion*
Why does Captain Wentworth eventually marry Anne and not Louisa?

ANITA BROOKNER: *Hotel du Lac*
Briefly describe David Simmonds, Geoffrey Long and Philip Neville. What kind of relationship did each offer Edith?

PAPER 3   USE OF ENGLISH   (2 hours)

SECTION A

1   *Fill each of the numbered blanks in the following passage with **one** suitable word.*

Chronic hunger and malnutrition represent the most compelling dilemma of our times. There are .... (1) simple solutions but there are signs of hope, perhaps the most important of these .... (2) the growing number of people .... (3) recognise the reality and nature of the interdependence .... (4) nations. This recognition of the vital links .... (5) the problems of food, trade and international finance was the impetus for establishing World Food Day.

The observance of World Food Day has encouraged .... (6) around the globe who share a commitment .... (7) eliminating hunger and malnutrition to focus on the needs of the poor. .... (8) to the statisticians the estimated .... (9) of people afflicted by hunger and malnutrition is about 500 million. But .... (10) alone do not begin to tell the real story of humiliation, sickness and suffering which that total represents.

Conditions facing the rural poor and the unemployed urban dweller are steadily .... (11) and little has been done to .... (12) their vulnerability to the impact of .... (13) harvests and natural calamities. Even more depressing is the prospect of over one and a half billion more people to be fed by the .... (14) 2000.

Nevertheless, a declaration put .... (15) by experts at the end of the World Food Day Colloquium .... (16) in Rome in October 1982 struck a cautiously optimistic .... (17). It read "More than ever before, humanity .... (18) the resources, capital, technology and

knowledge to promote development and to feed all people, both
.... (19) and in the foreseeable future. .... (20) the year
2000 the entire world population can be fed and nourished". We shall have
to wait and see.

2   *Finish each of the following sentences in such a way that it is as similar as possible
    in meaning to the sentence printed before it.*

    EXAMPLE: Immediately after his arrival things went wrong.

    ANSWER: No sooner *had he arrived than things went wrong.*

    a)   I only recognised him when he came into the light.
         Not until ....

    b)   That rumour about the politician and the construction contract is
         absolutely false.
         There is ....

    c)   One runner was too exhausted to complete the last lap of the race.
         One runner was so ....

    d)   My mother was the most warm-hearted person I've ever known.
         I've ....

    e)   They never made us do anything we didn't want to do.
         We ....

    f)   The only thing that prevented the passing of the bill was the death of
         the Prime Minister.
         Had it not ....

    g)   It is quite pointless to complain.
         There's no ....

3   *Fill each of the blanks with a suitable word or phrase.*

EXAMPLE: He doesn't mind one way or the other; it makes *no difference to* him.

a)   I called out his name three times, but he paid .... me.

b)   Don't lend your toys to Mary: she never .... borrow hers.

c)   It was .... a million that my cousin and I should run into each other in London.

d)   He should .... than to try and deceive the teacher.

e)   I wish .... advice as I can see now that you were quite right.

f)   Considering his .... experience, he is doing that job very well.

4   *For each of the sentences below, write a new sentence* **as similar as possible in meaning to the original sentence**, *but using the word given. This word* **must not be altered** *in any way.*

EXAMPLE: Not many people attended this meeting.
    turnout

ANSWER: *There was a poor turnout for the meeting.*

a)   You can't possibly expect me to have supper ready by 8 o'clock.
    question

    ....

b)   It is my opinion that there is no advantage in further discussion.
    see

    ....

c)   Please excuse Jane's poor typing: she's only been learning for a month.
    allowances

    ....

d) There is no way that young man can achieve success in this test.
    bound

    ....

e) Although the dog appeared harmless, it was, in fact, quite dangerous.
    contrary

    ....

f) If Smith hadn't broken his leg, he would have played football for
    England.
    represented

    ....

g) This hotel is inaccessible in winter.
    possible

    ....

h) As far as I know he is still working in Bristol.
    knowledge

    ....

SECTION B

5   *Read the following passage, then answer the questions which follow it.*

Sleeplessness

I spend the time when I ought to be asleep in worried reflection on the
mind/body problem, as philosophers call it. For that, to me, is what is at
issue during those white, bleary nights. Sleep is a gift, elusive because
gratuitous. It won't come when called: an inspiration of the body, it
ignores mental will. Insomnia teaches you how ill-matched mind and   5
body really are. The organism dislikes taking orders from its egotistic
owner, and relishes the chance for defiance. You spend hours of torment
before dawn raging at the body's obstinacy and stupidity, which merely
makes it more determined not to surrender.

Then you wonder whether you have chosen the right culprit. Which of   10
the two is responsible for your wakefulness? The body has done its
day's work and is ready for a spell of non-existence. It's the mind which
won't switch off, still fretting over unfinished business and fantasising

about the plots of your enemies. Insomnia seems like an early version of schizophrenia: you are confronted with the mutual mistrust and antago-   15
nism of your two main components.

Insomnia requires a scapegoat: it makes you blame yourself for something which isn't your fault. Meanwhile you are goaded to frenzies of jealousy against those who find the process so innocently facile: a contented snorer in the hotel room next door; even worse, someone in   20
bed beside you who is not suffering in sympathy. What saintly self-control it takes not to disturb the person sharing your bed. Rarely am I unselfish enough, and I've perfected a sigh which changes to a moan as my cry for help.

I also have a graduated list of remedies and rituals. Sparing myself, I   25
blame the bed, and, if possible, I transfer to another one. Even if I stay put, however, there's another possibility. I reverse the bedclothes and arrange myself with my feet at the headboard. I have a crackpot scientific justification for this. Someone once told me that you should sleep aligned with the magnetic field of the earth; flinging the blankets back   30
and forth, I can try out parallel and anti-parallel alignments. Of course, I have only the vaguest idea of what the earth's magnetic field is, and none at all about where it is. But the mind, by 3 am, is a sucker for any lie, and it sometimes works.

People say you should get up and clean out your cupboards or   35
reorganise your bookshelves. I can't bear to do any of this, because it makes me feel I'm a ghost returned to haunt myself, prowling through a house which looks deserted, unoccupied, estranged from its living daily purpose. Very occasionally I'll permit myself to read. It must be something which is uninteresting (otherwise I want to stay awake and   40
continue reading) without being boring. If reading fails me, I consider pills. I am too proud to ask the doctor for sedatives, so I hoard medicines from the hay-fever season for use all the year round. "May cause drowsiness", the packets teasingly half-promise, refusing to guarantee anything. Self-deception is the surest cure, and one of these pink   45
placebos convinces me that the problem has been taken care of (which, since the problem was imaginary all along, it probably has been).

Once you realise you won't sleep, the ordeal consists of passing the time. But time passes without you, while you remain suspended; and as the hours plod on, it starts to taunt you. I sleep below a clock in a tower,   50
which bangs out the numbers with concussing force and makes the room shudder. By day I never hear it. After midnight, every stroke is a personal reproof – another hour used up, with no sleep to show for it.

Why, I'm regularly reduced to wondering, is sleep something I'm so bad at? I envy dictators, creatures of will who are self-advertising   55
insomniacs: Napoleon was painted in his study among guttering candles, with the curtains drawn and the clock hands at 17 minutes past 4. The emperor doesn't look at all tired.

a)   ". . . an inspiration of the body, it ignores mental will" (lines 4–5). What does the author mean when he says this?

....

....

b)   What is "the organism", and in what way does it "relish the chance for defiance" (lines 6–7)?

....

....

c)   What are "your two main components" and how through insomnia are you "confronted with their mutual mistrust and antagonism" (lines 15–16)?

....

....

....

d)   Why does insomnia require a scapegoat?

....

....

e)   What is the author "rarely . . . unselfish enough" to do (lines 22–23)?

....

f)   Explain the phrase "Sparing myself, I blame the bed" (lines 25–26).

....

....

g)   Explain the phrase "stay put" in the context of the passage (lines 26–27).

....

h) What "scientific justification" does the author give for sleeping with his feet at the headboard and why is this described as "crackpot" (lines 28–29)?

....

....

....

i) What does the author mean when he says that "the mind, by 3 am, is a sucker for any lie" (lines 33–34)?

....

....

j) Why should the author feel like "a ghost returned to haunt myself" (line 37)?

....

k) Why does the author hoard medicines for use all the year round?

....

....

....

l) In what way do the medicine packets refuse to guarantee anything, and what is meant by "Self-deception is the surest cure" (line 45)?

....

....

....

m) What is meant by "creature of will"? On what evidence does the author describe Napoleon as a "self-advertising insomniac" (lines 55–56)?

....

....

....

n) In a paragraph of 70–90 words explain what the author suggests may be the cause of his insomnia and describe the ways in which he tries to overcome it.

....

....

....

....

....

....

....

....

....

....

....

....

PAPER 4   LISTENING COMPREHENSION
(about 30 minutes)

PART ONE

You will hear a radio programme about an airline company and its relations with some of its employees. For each of the questions 1–10, tick the box if the statement is one of the reasons why the stewardesses felt discriminated against. If it is not, leave the box blank.

1   They were paid less than the men for the same work.

2   They had to wait years to become pursers.

3   They had to watch their weight.

4   They sometimes didn't get paid.

5   They were made to share a room on over-night stops.

6   They faced compulsory retirement at 42.

7   They had to be of a certain height.

8   They had to carry regulation luggage.

9   They lost their job if they married.

10   They had to work very long hours.

PART TWO

You will hear a young girl discussing legal rights. For each of the questions 11–19, tick a 'Yes' or 'No' box to indicate which activities are legal at the age of 16.

	Yes	No
11 join the army		
12 donate blood		
13 obtain a passport		
14 marry		
15 sign a contract		
16 be sued for debt		
17 vote		
18 get a Saturday job		
19 buy alcohol		

PART THREE

You will hear part of a radio news item about the Lee View housing estate.
For each of the questions 20–25, tick one of the boxes A, B, C or D to show the correct
answer.

20 On the day the recording was made,

    A tenants moved into their modernised homes.

    B new tenants were moving into the estate.

    C the buildings were being modernised.

    D the architects showed people their new homes.

A	
B	
C	
D	

21 When Mickey Lewis first moved to the estate, he

    A wasn't completely satisfied.

    B was extremely popular.

    C didn't like it at all.

    D wanted it to be redecorated.

A	
B	
C	
D	

22 What caused the estate to deteriorate?

    A Repairs had not been carried out.

    B The tenants had no money.

    C It was constructed of poor quality materials.

    D There were unscrupulous private landlords.

A	
B	
C	
D	

23 While modernisation was taking place, what happened to the tenants?

    A They were moved into private accommodation.

    B They were moved into hotels.

    C They went to another council estate.

    D They remained on the same estate.

A	
B	
C	
D	

24 The architect says that dealing with the tenants was

    A   an unacceptable situation.

    B   an experience he does not want to repeat.

    C   a stimulating experience.

    D   a dull task.

A	
B	
C	
D	

25 In the new design, where do families live?

    A   On the third floor.

    B   On the ground floor.

    C   In detached houses.

    D   In carpeted flats.

A	
B	
C	
D	

PAPER 5   INTERVIEW   (15–20 minutes)

You will be asked to take part in a conversation with a group of other students or with your teacher. The conversation will be based on one particular topic area or theme, for example holidays, work, food.

Of course each interview will be different for each student or group of students, but a *typical* interview is described below.

* At the start of the interview you will be asked to talk about one of the photographs among the Interview Exercises at the back of the book.

* You will then be asked to discuss one of the passages at the back of the book. Your teacher may ask you to talk about its content, where you think it comes from, who the author or speaker is, whether you agree or disagree with it, and so on. You will *not* be asked to read the passage aloud, but you may quote parts of it to make your point.

* You may then be asked to discuss for example an advertisement, a leaflet, extract from a newspaper etc. Your teacher will tell you which of the Interview Exercises to look at.

* You may also be asked to take part in an activity with a group of other students or your teacher. Your teacher will tell you which section among the Interview Exercises you should look at.

Practice Test 3

PAPER 1   READING COMPREHENSION   (1 hour)

Answer all questions. Indicate your choice of answer in every case **on the separate answer sheet** *already given out, which should show your name and examination index number. Follow carefully the instructions about how to record your answers. Give* **one answer only** *to each question. Marks will not be deducted for wrong answers: your total score on this test will be the number of correct answers you give.*

SECTION A

In this section you must choose the word or phrase which best completes each sentence. **On your answer sheet** *indicate the letter A, B, C or D against the number of each item 1 to 25 for the word or phrase you choose.*

1   Sparkling pools of water lay trapped among the rocks as the tide ....
    A removed   B refilled   C retired   D receded

2   The purpose of the survey was to .... the inspectors with local conditions.
    A inform   B acquaint   C instruct   D notify

3   He was disqualified for failing to .... with the rules of the competition.
    A accommodate   B compete   C comply   D acquiesce

4   He realised that the manager was angry from the .... tone he adopted.
    A brief   B smooth   C curt   D high

5   Frank would be more popular in the office if he didn't try so hard to .... himself with the boss.
    A regard   B sympathise   C congratulate   D ingratiate

6   This man is so arrogant that he is completely .... to all criticism.
    A impervious   B unaware   C regardless   D unconscious

7   The recent economic crisis has brought about a .... in world trade.
    A slump   B sag   C droop   D tilt

8   When we went to Egypt he knew .... no Arabic, but within six months he had become extremely fluent.
    A entirely   B virtually   C barely   D scarcely

9   The old lady's savings were considerable as she had .... a little money each week.
    A put by   B put in   C put apart   D put down

10 His poor handling of the business .... on negligence.
    A bordered   B edged   C approached   D neared

11 After the accident, there was considerable doubt .... exactly what had happened.
    A in the question of   B as to   C in the shape of   D for

12 Price increases are now running at a(n) .... level of thirty per cent.
    A highest   B record   C uppermost   D top

13 The police .... a good deal of criticism over their handling of the demonstration.
    A came in for   B brought about   C went down with   D opened up

14 Whenever we plan to go for a picnic, it .... rains.
    A continuously   B invariably   C unavoidably   D interminably

15 If you are .... of hearing, you will find our hearing aids invaluable.
    A short   B hard   C poor   D weak

16 I know you didn't want to upset me but I'd sooner you .... me the whole truth yesterday.
    A tell   B told   C have told   D had told

17 The prospective buyer had decided to look .... the property before committing himself.
    A about   B out   C over   D up

18 I didn't really want to see the film, but my wife was so .... to go that I finally agreed.
    A willing   B sincere   C keen   D energetic

19 Send for our free brochure by .... the coupon below.
    A answering   B responding   C completing   D filling

20 The judge imposed a light sentence in view of the .... circumstances.
    A unfair   B extensive   C extenuating   D qualifying

21 His parents' hostile attitude .... him to leave home.
    A drove   B urged   C made   D suggested

22 No sooner had he sat down to lunch .... there was a knock at the door.
    A when   B that   C as   D than

23 The students visited the museum and spent several hours with the ....,
who was very helpful.
A commissioner   B bursar   C steward   D curator

24 Despite his knowledge of climbing techniques, he was not considered
.... to lead the expedition.
A reliable   B experienced   C competent   D responsible

25 I have absolutely no .... of the conversation you refer to.
A reminiscence   B reminder   C recall   D recollection

SECTION B

*In this section you will find after each of the passages a number of questions or
unfinished statements about the passage, each with four suggested answers or ways of
finishing. You must choose the one which you think fits best according to the passage.*
On your answer sheet, *indicate the letter A, B, C or D against the number of each
item 26–40 for the answer you choose. Give* **one answer only** *to each question. Read
each passage right through before choosing your answers.*

FIRST PASSAGE

Trevor King and I had worked together for six years, ever since he'd enticed me
from the city office where I'd been trained with the one inducement I couldn't
refuse: flexible working hours which allowed time to go racing. He already had
five or six clients from the racing world, Newbury being central for many of the
racing stables strung out along the Berkshire Downs, and, needing a replace-
ment for a departing assistant, he'd reckoned that if he engaged me he might
acquire a good deal more business in that direction. Not that he'd ever actually
said so, because he was not a man to use two words where one would do; but
his open satisfaction as his plan had gradually worked made it obvious.
 All he had apparently done towards checking my ability as an accountant, as
opposed to amateur jockey, was to ask my former employers if they would offer
me a substantial raise in salary in order to keep me. They said yes, and did so.
Trevor, it seemed, had smiled like a great shark, and gone away. His subse-
quent offer to me had been for a full partnership and lots of racing time; the
partnership would cost me ten thousand pounds and I could pay it to him over
several years out of my earnings. What did I think?
 I'd thought it might turn out just fine; and it had.
 In some ways I knew Trevor no better than on that first day. Our real
relationship began and ended at the office door, social contact outside being
confined to one formal dinner party each year, to which I was invited by letter
by his wife.
 On the professional level, I knew him well. Orthodox establishment outlook,

sober and traditional. Patriarchal, but not pompous. Giving the sort of gilt-edged advice that still appeared sound even if in hindsight it turned out not to be.

Something punitive about him, perhaps. He seemed to me sometimes to get a positive pleasure from detailing the extent of a client's tax liabilities, and watching the client droop.

Precise in mind and method, discreetly ambitious, pleased to be a noted local personage, and at his charming best with rich old ladies. His favourite clients were prosperous companies; his least favourite, incompetent individuals with their affairs in a mess.

26 Why was the writer offered a partnership?
    A   He was an excellent accountant.
    B   He could work long hours.
    C   He had useful contacts.
    D   King's business was in difficulty.

27 Why did the writer accept King's offer?
    A   He didn't like his employers.
    B   He could choose when to work.
    C   He wanted to help King
    D   The partnership was a bargain.

28 How did King and the writer get on together?
    A   They were close friends.
    B   They had frequent disagreements.
    C   They had a successful working relationship.
    D   They had very little contact at work.

29 What type of businessman was King?
    A   clever
    B   dishonest
    C   incompetent
    D   generous

30 What do we learn about King in his job?
    A   He felt sorry for clients with problems.
    B   His advice was always correct.
    C   He adopted a modern approach.
    D   He enjoyed giving clients bad news.

31 To whom did King behave charmingly?
    A   colleagues
    B   clients in trouble
    C   prominent local figures
    D   wealthy old ladies

SECOND PASSAGE

"He is an old woman"; "poor old dear'; "she's past it" – who has not used such phrases? Most of us do without thinking twice about it. If younger people are "senile", it means they are beyond hope and can be dismissed as too feeble to contribute anything.

This language of derision or ridicule is only one of the facets of the most pervasive prejudice in our society and one which seems to be growing: ageism. Ageism means assessing a person's worth solely by their age. Some people will not suffer directly from the best known "isms" of today: sexism and racism. But everyone is a potential victim of ageism and all of us are guilty of perpetrating it.

We are guilty because, just as racism and sexism operate against people with a particular skin colour or gender, so society has developed a systematic process of stereotyping and discriminating against people because they are old.

The stereotype imposed upon older people is a cruel one. When you are old you are not allowed the same feelings and needs as you had in your youth; love and jealousy are regarded as ludicrous; sexuality repulsive; violence ridiculous.

Society expects you to be an example of the virtues, especially serenity and wisdom, but at the same time you are dismissed, patronised and treated as a fool. You hear that retirement is a time of freedom and leisure, but the majority have such a poor standard of living that it is difficult or impossible to enjoy that freedom.

Older women face extra problems men may not have, since ageing for women in our society is viewed as a loss of sexual attractiveness and a magnification of all the prejudices that women always come across. No wonder that loss of self-esteem often follows.

If a visitor from outer space were to sit in front of the TV screen and watch commercials for a day, he/she would conclude that the human race was made up of men and an attractive sub-species of creatures under the age of thirty. That is because older women are virtually invisible in advertisements. Understandably, young and pretty models add appeal, but don't older women buy products too? Unfortunately at the end of the day advertising only plays back images already in the public's mind and reflects our prejudices.

32　Why does the writer consider "ageism" harmful?
    A　It judges all old people by the same criteria.
    B　We will all eventually suffer from it.
    C　It has a bad effect on language.
    D　It prevents old people contributing to society.

33　The author suggests that we deny that old people can
    A　have emotional experiences.
    B　feel youthful.
    C　enjoy sexual equality.
    D　experience individual freedom.

34 Which of these characteristics do we expect in old people?
   A stupidity
   B calmness
   C laziness
   D humility

35 Why does the author think that "ageism" is more of a problem for women?
   A They are too poor to enjoy their retirement.
   B A woman's appearance deteriorates more quickly than a man's.
   C People find old women less pleasant to look at.
   D Women are less confident than men.

THIRD PASSAGE

There are those whom we instantly recognise as clinging to the traditional values of travel, the people who endure a kind of alienation and panic in foreign parts for the after-taste of having sampled new scenes. On the whole, travel at its best is rather comfortless, but travel is never easy: you get very tired, you get lost, you get your feet wet, you get little co-operation, and – if it is to have any value at all – you go alone. Homesickness is part of this kind of travel. In these circumstances, it is possible to make interesting discoveries about oneself and one's surroundings. Travel has less to do with distance than with insight: it is, very often, a way of seeing.

The second group of travellers has only appeared in numbers in the past twenty years. For these people, paradoxically, travel is an experience of familiar things; it is travel that carries with it the illusion of immobility. It is going to a familiar airport and being strapped into a seat and held captive for a number of hours – immobile; then arriving at an almost identical airport; being whisked to a hotel so fast it is not like movement at all, and the hotel and the food are identical to the hotel and the food in the city one has just left. This is all tremendously reassuring and effortless; indeed, it is possible to go from – say – London to Singapore and not experience the feeling of having travelled anywhere.

For many years in the past, this was enjoyed by the rich. It is wrong to call it tourism, because businessmen also travel this way; and many people, who believe themselves to be travellers, object to being called tourists. The luxury travellers of the past set an example for the package tourists of today. In this sort of travel you take your society with you: your language, your food, your styles of hotel and service. It is of course the prerogative of rich nations – America, Western Europe, and Japan. It has had a profound effect on our view of the world. It has made real travel greatly sought after and somewhat rare. And I think it has caused a resurgence of travel writing.

As everyone knows, travel is very unsettling, and it can be quite hazardous and worrying. One way of overcoming this anxiety is to travel packaged in style: luxury is a great remedy for the alienation of travel. What helps calm us is a reminder of stability and protection – and what the average package tourist looks for in foreign surroundings is familiar sights.

36 The travellers described in paragraph 1
    A travel great distances.
    B are afraid of new experiences.
    C learn a lot about new places.
    D receive more help from local people.

37 According to the author, the "traditional" traveller
    A feels at home in new places.
    B enjoys minor discomforts.
    C should expect to feel homesick.
    D dislikes company.

38 The author suggests that the second group of travellers
    A chooses boring destinations.
    B is afraid of anything new.
    C would prefer to stay at home.
    D adapts quickly to fresh surroundings.

39 What gives travel an "illusion of immobility"? (line 12)
    A the absence of new experiences
    B the onset of fatigue
    C the number of people travelling
    D the length of the journey

40 Which of the following statements best sums up the author's attitude to travel?
    A Travel has to be tiring to be worthwhile.
    B The package holiday encourages interest in new places.
    C Modern travel has become comfortable but boring.
    D Only the rich can travel in comfort.

PAPER 2   COMPOSITION   (2 hours)

*Write **two only** of the following composition exercises. Your answers must follow exactly the instructions given. Write in pen, not pencil. You are allowed to make alterations, but see that your work is clear and easy to read.*

1   Describe how your experiences have helped to develop your character. (About 350 words)

2   There is a saying: "Money can't buy happiness, but it can help!" Do you agree? (About 350 words)

3   Write a story which begins or ends: "Home at last!" (About 350 words)

4   Your friends have accepted an invitation to come and stay in your house while you and your family are away. Write a letter giving them all the information necessary to make their visit enjoyable and trouble-free. (About 300 words)

5   Basing your answer on your reading of the prescribed text concerned, answer **one** of the following. (About 350 words)

GRAHAM GREENE: *The Quiet American*
Write an account of the relationship between Fowler and Pyle.

JANE AUSTEN: *Persuasion*
"Jane Austen's main theme throughout the novel is one of love and marriage." Discuss this statement.

ANITA BROOKNER: *Hotel du Lac*
"Edith Hope's relationships with men are the most important aspects of the novel." Discuss.

PAPER 3   USE OF ENGLISH   (2 hours)

SECTION A

1   *Fill each of the numbered blanks in the following passage with* **one** *suitable word.*

Until the nineteenth century, the ownership of land was the only certain basis of power in England. It is true that both power and money .... (1) be acquired by .... (2) means: by trade, by commerce, by fighting, by useful services to the government or by personal service to the king and queen. But .... (3) unsupported by power was .... (4) to be plundered, power based only on personal abilities was at the .... (5) of time and fortune, and the power to be .... (6) through trade or commerce was limited. Before the nineteenth century .... (7) wealth of England lay in the .... (8) as opposed to the towns; landowners .... (9) than merchants were the dominating .... (10) and ran the country .... (11) that their own interests were the .... (12) to suffer. Even .... (13) the economic balance began to change, they were so thoroughly in .... (14) of administration and legislation, ... (15) their political and social supremacy continued. As a .... (16), from the Middle Ages until the nineteenth century, ... (17) who had made money by whatever .... (18), and was ambitious for .... (19) and his family, automatically invested .... (20) a country estate.

2 *Finish each of the following sentences in such a way that it means exactly the same as the sentence printed before it.*

EXAMPLE: Immediately after his arrival things went wrong.

ANSWER: No sooner *had he arrived than things went wrong.*

a) The workers only called off the strike after a new pay offer.

Only after ....

b) He was sentenced to six months in prison for his part in the robbery.

He received a ....

c) You can eat as much as you like for £5 at the new lunch-bar.

There is no ....

d) She wore a hearing-aid, even though she could hear the phone ring perfectly well.

She wasn't so ....

e) You will never meet anyone more generous than Mrs Jones.

Mrs Jones is ....

f) My parents let me go abroad alone for the first time last year.

I was ....

g) It was his incompetence which led to their capture.

If ....

h) I'm certainly not going to give you any more money.

I have no ....

3 *Fill each of the blanks with a suitable word or phrase.*

EXAMPLE: He doesn't mind one way or the other; it makes *no difference to* him.

a) It never .... me that he might be lying.

b) He tiptoed into the room .... waken his wife.

c) You must come in the summer because my roses are at .... then.

d) You'd better .... start to avoid the worst of the traffic.

e) She looked such a fool with her hair dyed green that I just
.... laughing at her.

f) There's no point in trying to explain it to her; she's ....
understanding.

4 *For each of the sentences below, write a new sentence* **as similar as possible in meaning to the original sentence**, *but using the word given. This word* **must not be altered in any way**.

EXAMPLE: Not many people attended the meeting.
turnout

ANSWER: *There was a poor turnout for the meeting.*

a) I don't think there will be any applicants for this post.
likelihood

....

b) It was difficult for Susan to believe the good news.
hardly

....

c) You must make allowances for his inexperience.
account

....

....

d) This contract is not binding until we both sign it.
bound

....

e) He wasn't to blame for the accident.
fault

....

f) You shouldn't take his help for granted.
assume

....

SECTION B

5   *Read the following passage, then answer the questions which follow it.*

National treasures

The sale by the University of Manchester of certain books from the
financially exhausted John Rylands Library has caused widespread
indignation. So too has the Government's proposed legislation per-
mitting national museums and galleries to sell works in their collections.

This is wholly understandable. No one likes the idea of selling family   5
heirlooms, even when they are dull, ugly things which very few actually
want to see. This has nothing to do with the question. Everyone feels
better for knowing that they are in the cellar. Sometimes they are of
particular emotional value – when they are in languages we cannot
understand, or their acquisition is associated with a romantic legend of   10
piracy or fraud.

One trouble with cellars, however, is their tendency to be damp.
Another is that if the family has been distinguished for several centuries
by its wealth, power and artistic taste, after the third century or so the
cellars begin to get rather crowded. If you have so much that you no   15
longer even know what you do have, and visit your cellars very
infrequently, you may find on your next incursion that time has worked
its wicked inartistic way with your priceless bins of art.

This is the trouble with the British Museum and the Victoria and
Albert Museum in London. Both were accused in a recent report of   20
scandalously neglecting the millions of works which lie unexhibited in
their collections. Many items are said to be already beyond repair. The
task of saving others would swallow more than the museums' entire
annual budget.

Meanwhile, there are millionaires in America – and, increasingly, in   25
Asia – who would cheerfully pay fortunes for many of these works, and
would exhibit or at least preserve them. Surely then, the sensible thing
would be to sell some of them, for the greater good of the majority?

There are, however, one or two arguments against such sales which
are worth considering. In the first place, it is said, this is the slippery   30
slope to a time when the Government will reckon that galleries can
support themselves by these means, and will cut subsidies still further.
Desperate galleries will then start raffling off their treasures to cover
current expenses. This would of course be a disaster.

The profit from sales must be spent only on purchase of new works or   35
restoration of old ones. The level of state funding should not change in
response to sales. Secondly, it is said, these works must be kept for
reasons of scholarship. In the Rylands Library case, the books were said
to be unnecessary second copies but they were not "duplicates" in the
strictest sense. Scholars need to be able to lay them side by side to study 40
their differences. Scholars, however, have modern reproduction tech-

niques available to them, and in most cases have no choice but to compare works that are thousands of miles apart. They will have to lump it.

Thirdly, it is argued, works have been bequeathed to the museums   45
concerned. To sell them would be illegal, or at least a breach of trust. The answer to this is that not showing works bequeathed is in any case an implicit breach of trust. To sell off the whole of a particular bequest would be wrong. To sell off some of it to save – and be able to display – the rest is quite justifiable. The prospect of such sales might also ensure   50
that givers as well as receivers pay attention to the costs as well as the benefits of keeping a precious collection intact.

Lastly, it is argued, no one can know at a given time whether in fifty or a hundred years a work now considered minor may not suddenly be recognised as a masterpiece. It must be recognised, however, that the   55
works concerned are hardly likely to be destroyed; they will still be available for study and reproduction.

There should certainly be some reticence about selling works by British artists, or ones by artists few of whose works exist in Britain. But museums cannot possibly hang onto every work of art they possess –   60
especially in view of the tendency of our age to swoon for an ever shorter time over what is fashionable, then wake up and forget about it, leaving last year's masterpiece to lie gathering dust.

The melancholy truth is that Britain acquired many of its art treasures when it was the richest country the world had ever seen. The world now   65
sees many richer – and the finances of museums and galleries reflect this.

a)   According to the writer what is "wholly understandable" (line 5)?

    ....

    ....

b)   "This has nothing to do with the question" (line 7). What is "the question" referred to?

    ....

    ....

c)   What are the factors that are said to give value to heirlooms?

    ....

    ....

d) Explain briefly the phrase ". . . time has worked its wicked inartistic way with your priceless bins of art" (lines 17–18).

....

....

e) Explain why the writer suggests that it would be sensible to sell off some works of art.

....

....

....

f) Why does the writer use the term "slippery slope" (lines 30–31) to describe the process of selling off art treasures?

....

....

g) Why might a gallery become "desperate" (line 33)?

....

....

h) Why does the writer oppose the argument for retaining certain books in the John Rylands Library?

....

....

....

i) What do you understand by the expression "They will have to lump it" (lines 43–44)?

....

....

j) In what way might a museum be guilty of "an implicit breach of trust" (lines 47–48)?

....

....

k) What argument does the writer use to justify breaking up a collection?

....

....

l) What precisely does the writer mean by the word "masterpiece" in line 55?

....

....

m) Why does the writer consider the "truth" to be "melancholy" (line 64)?

....

....

n) Summarise, in a paragraph of 50–60 words, the arguments the writer uses to support the proposed sale of works from national museums and galleries.

....

....

....

....

....

....

....

....

PAPER 4 LISTENING COMPREHENSION
(about 30 minutes)

PART ONE

You will hear a conversation between two people who have just missed a train.
For each of the questions 1–5, tick one of the boxes A, B, C or D to show the correct
answer.

1 At the beginning of the conversation the tone of the man's voice
  suggests he is

  A forgiving.

  B calm.

  C angry.

  D offhand.

A	
B	
C	
D	

2 When the man refers to things that have happened in the past,
  he is being

  A sarcastic.

  B considerate.

  C encouraging.

  D suspicious.

A	
B	
C	
D	

3 When the man says ". . . grown woman", he is

  A suggesting she should do more on her own initiative.

  B hinting that she is not as young as she used to be.

  C marvelling at her maturity.

  D insinuating that she is overweight.

A	
B	
C	
D	

4   When the man says "Mm, I suppose so", he is agreeing that

    A   the flat is too small to accommodate them.

    B   staying in a hotel would cost too much.

    C   they have not got the right money for the phone.

    D   it would be inconsiderate to phone her friends now.

A	
B	
C	
D	

5   The second time the man says "Worcester", he

    A   is agreeing with the woman's suggestion.

    B   is wondering whether it appears on the timetable.

    C   thinks he has solved the problem.

    D   has rejected it as a serious possibility.

A	
B	
C	
D	

PART TWO

You will hear an extract from a radio programme about vaccination against measles. For each of the questions 6–15, tick one box to show whether the statement is true or false.

	True	False
6 Measles vaccine can now be given using a foot pump.		
7 Initially the live virus vaccine was given by injection.		
8 Dr Ibrahim invented the new method of giving the vaccine.		
9 The person who gives the vaccine has to wear a mask over his mouth and nose.		
10 It is difficult to know when the child has had enough vaccine.		
11 The pump that they use is quite sophisticated.		
12 The live vaccine can be kept in a thermos flask.		
13 With the new method sterilisers are unnecessary.		
14 With the new method a doctor must give the vaccine.		
15 Dr Ibrahim believes that everybody will have been vaccinated against measles within three or four years.		

PART THREE

You will hear a telephone information service giving horoscopes. Below are six horoscopes and six star signs. For each star sign there is one horoscope. For questions 16–21, write the letter of the corresponding horoscope in the box beside the star sign.

Horoscopes

a   Think before losing your temper.
b   Avoid making any long term plans.
c   Go dancing and have a good time.
d   Make good a broken promise.
e   Avoid interfering in other people's affairs.
f   Remain cool and calm.

16   Leo   16   C

17   Virgo   17

18   Libra   18

19   Scorpio   19

20   Sagittarius 20

21   Capricorn   21

PAPER 5   INTERVIEW   (15–20 minutes)

You will be asked to take part in a conversation with a group of other students or with your teacher. The conversation will be based on one particular topic area or theme, for example holidays, work, food.

Of course each interview will be different for each student or group of students, but a *typical* interview is described below.

* At the start of the interview you will be asked to talk about one of the photographs among the Interview Exercises at the back of the book.

* You will then be asked to discuss one of the passages at the back of the book. Your teacher may ask you to talk about its content, where you think it comes from, who the author or speaker is, whether you agree or disagree with it, and so on. You will *not* be asked to read the passage aloud, but you may quote parts of it to make your point.

* You may then be asked to discuss for example an advertisement, a leaflet, extract from a newspaper etc. Your teacher will tell you which of the Interview Exercises to look at.

* You may also be asked to take part in an activity with a group of other students or your teacher. Your teacher will tell you which section among the Interview Exercises you should look at.

Practice Test 4

PAPER 1   READING COMPREHENSION   (1 hour)

Answer all questions. Indicate your choice of answer in every case **on the separate answer sheet** *already given out, which should show your name and examination index number. Follow carefully the instructions about how to record your answers. Give* **one answer only** *to each question. Marks will not be deducted for wrong answers: your total score on this test will be the number of correct answers you give.*

SECTION A

In this section you must choose the word or phrase which best completes each sentence. **On your answer sheet** *indicate the letter A, B, C or D against the number of each item 1 to 25 for the word or phrase you choose.*

1   The police have been ordered not to .... if the students attack them.
    A combat   B retaliate   C challenge   D rebuff

2   The organisers of the competition are unable to .... into any discussion of the results.
    A embark   B enter   C undertake   D negotiate

3   The dampness of the walls caused the paint to .... off.
    A crumble   B splinter   C flake   D scale

4   .... the government fall, the stock market will crash.
    A Provided   B In case   C Should   D Had

5   The politician tried to arouse the crowd, but most of them were .... to his arguments.
    A closed   B dead   C careless   D indifferent

6   For elderly people, one of the problems .... by rising prices is the continual increase in heating bills.
    A given   B posed   C pressed   D forced

7   Both her novels can lay some .... to being classics of modern literature.
    A right   B claim   C foundation   D notion

8   Many buildings which are currently in disuse could be .... to other
    purposes.
    A changed   B employed   C used   D put

9   The price they offered for my old car was so low that I .... it down.
    A turned   B brought   C called   D shouted

10 When we got to the box office the question of who should pay ....
    A raised   B arose   C came   D appeared

11 The police car set off in .... of the robbers.
    A pursuit   B prosecution C chase   D trail

12 It was felt that the new bonus for increased production would provide an
    .... to work overtime.
    A incitement B attraction   C initiative   D incentive

13 We're rather short of people to organise the trip, so do you think you could
    .... ?
    A take on   B join up   C fix up   D help out

14 Candidates should note that the .... for entries for the examination is
    2nd December.
    A deadline   B term   C period   D closure

15 .... that he passes all his exams first time, he'll be qualified in under
    four years.
    A Considering B Assuming   C Hoping   D Speculating

16 Everyone in the village .... it difficult to resist the stranger's charming
    smile.
    A made   B had   C found   D felt

17 If you would like a larger print of your photograph we can blow it ....
    for you.
    A out   B through   C up   D over

18 A solution to the problem of widespread tax evasion is long ....
    A postponed   B overdrawn   C overdue   D outstanding

19 It would be helpful if you could .... the report into three or four pages.
    A resume   B decrease   C reduce   D condense

20 I was surprised when he swore at me as vulgarity is .... to his nature.
    A opposed   B foreign   C contrasted D different

21 The government's new safety pamphlet .... against smoking in bed.
    A declares   B advises   C emphasises   D stresses

22 He can't even speak his own language properly, ... Spanish.
    A without saying   B leaving out   C let alone   D to mention

23 The driver .... his greatest ambition by winning the Grand Prix.
    A obtained   B confirmed   C realised   D completed

24 He was told he could join the Scouts when he .... old enough.
    A would be   B should be   C was   D were

25 The 10% rise in the cost of living is almost unbelievable until one looks at it
    in the .... of world price rises.
    A significance   B relationship   C situation   D context

SECTION B

*In this section you will find after each of the passages a number of questions or
unfinished statements about the passage, each with four suggested answers or ways of
finishing. You must choose the one which you think fits best according to the passage.*
On your answer sheet, *indicate the letter A, B, C or D against the number of each
item 26–40 for the answer you choose. Give* **one answer only** *to each question. Read
each passage right through before choosing your answers.*

FIRST PASSAGE

There was a note on the desk informing me that Mr Sumner, journalist, would
be arriving during the night. I was to show him around the factory, allowing
him to see anything and anyone.

"You'd think," I said to Sid, who shared the room with me and who was
resting his feet on the desk, "that I had nothing better to do."

He turned out to be plump, Mr Sumner, and he wore an expensive grey suit.
Over his arm he carried a new pair of overalls. As soon as he was in the room he
smiled charmingly at both of us and shook us by the hand. Sid, ironically
courteous, offered Sumner his seat and himself sat on a tin can in the corner of
the room. Sumner immediately offered cigarettes. We only took one each.

"I hope," Sumner began, "that I am not putting you out at all." He enlarged
his smile and looked at us both steadily, in turn. "My idea, basically, is to look
at industry from the other side. One has the management's point of view, of
course. But I want to know," the white, plump hand circling the face, as if he
was hypnotising himself and falling with the italicised word "how the *worker*
feels about industry."

"Exhausted," said Sid. "Most of the time," he added.

Sumner laughed. His laugh like his voice was steady and soft, discreet, establishing mutual sympathy and understanding. He behaved and looked like a visitor from a distant place where elegance was not the mark of a traitor.

"That is the kind of thing I want," he said.

Above the noise of the cranes as they passed the window we could hear a wail, beginning like one cat in pain but growing until it might have been ten in a variety of agonies. Sumner jumped in his seat and dropped his cigarette. He was going to stamp on it but I picked it up and gave it to him and he put it back in his mouth. The door was kicked open and Lennie, who had been making the noise, came in swearing. Sumner could not hide his astonishment at Lennie's appearance, at the red hair to the shoulders, the lens-less spectacles, the red, six-inch-long nose, the black, heavy moustache.

"Lennie," I said, "meet Mr Sumner, a writer for the papers."

"Thank God," said Lennie, taking his spectacles off. Since the false nose and moustache were attached to them they also came off. He removed the wig. Lennie was grey-haired and solemn-faced; his nose was still abnormally long. "Pardon me," he said to Sumner, "I thought you were one of these fancy managers. No offence."

26 What was the purpose of Sumner's visit?
    A   to bring information from the management.
    B   to check the efficiency of the workers.
    C   to find out the attitude of the workers.
    D   to examine the machinery at the factory.

27 What was the narrator's reaction to the proposed visit?
    A   He thought it would be a waste of his time.
    B   He was pleased to have something different to do.
    C   He was happy to assist the management.
    D   He thought it would cause trouble.

28 When Sumner arrived Sid's behaviour was
    A   hostile.
    B   polite.
    C   nervous.
    D   indifferent.

29 Sumner's manner of speaking showed him to be
    A   a stranger to this environment.
    B   an inexperienced journalist.
    C   a prejudiced reporter.
    D   a man who could not be trusted.

30 What does Lennie's behaviour suggest?
    A He did not like journalists.
    B He did not like managers.
    C He wanted to surprise Sid.
    D He was a cheerful person.

SECOND PASSAGE

Television, like language, can be a cultural challenge for better or worse, and this is what it is in many of its activities, whether voluntarily or, on occasion, involuntarily. Although it may sometimes be soothing, television is often provocative in the sense that it gives information and arouses interest. That being said, the new means of broadcasting and communicating throughout the world increases the complexity of television even further.

An important question is what television is there to do and to say. In actual fact, however, the issue does not seem to have been put in this way by all governments and their officials, nor by private television companies.

Since the primary aim is to get an audience (and who would want to make television programmes nobody looked at?), programmes are becoming more and more standardised. The cultural challenge represented by television must not turn into a challenge to culture. At all events, television carries messages which influence, and will increasingly influence, trends in our societies one way or another. Either television will contribute to enriching our cultures or it will contribute to eroding them or to enabling some of these cultures to dominate others.

Undoubtedly there are outstanding events, such as broadcasts of major occasions, but the out-of-the-ordinary nature of a cultural message soon becomes part of life, part of the very air breathed by those to whom the messages are sent. Living in a world of painting, literature and music is a very different thing from the stardom of a composer, writer or performer. While the heads of television channels sometimes display boldness, they do not seem to find it necessary to do so when it comes to music (with the occasional exception), because they themselves are not convinced of the emotional impact of music on television. And yet, in spite of all obstacles, music is a challenge through its daily presence. This represents a victory for whom? Pure music – that is to say, music soberly presented through the playing of the performers – goes down very well on the small screen. Its presence on television makes it part of everyday life.

Let us be optimistic and hope that those in charge of television of whatever kind are aware of the importance of their function over and above audience surveys and ratings and that they will call primarily on the talents of cultural people and give them priority over the salesman.

31   What is the effect of television according to the author?
    A   It causes intellectual laziness.
    B   It makes the viewers think.
    C   It is harmful to society.
    D   It confuses the viewers.

32   In the author's opinion, what is wrong with the attitude of some
    governments to television?
    A   They do not think it is important.
    B   They do not pay enough attention to its function.
    C   They do not use it effectively.
    D   They have too much control over it.

33   The author thinks that television programmes are in danger of
    A   trying to please too many people.
    B   preventing the development of society.
    C   losing their effect on our culture.
    D   declining in popularity.

34   According to the author, the heads of television channels
    A   have an adventurous approach to presenting music.
    B   broadcast only important musical events.
    C   do not think music is effective on television.
    D   do not want music to be part of everyday life.

35   What does the author hope will be the future of television?
    A   More popular programmes will be broadcast.
    B   Television controllers will change their attitudes.
    C   Audiences will go on increasing.
    D   The right kind of programme-makers will be appointed.

THIRD PASSAGE

Opinion poll surveys show that the public see scientists in a rather unflattering
light. They are seen as cold, humourless, remote and unwilling (or unable) to
communicate their specialised knowledge to ordinary people.

Commonly, the scientist is also seen as being male: the characteristics listed
above are popularly associated with "maleness". It is true that most scientists
are male, but the picture of science as a male activity may be a major reason why
fewer girls than boys opt for science, except when it comes to biology, which is
seen as "female".

The image most people have of science and scientists comes from their own
experience of school science, and from the mass media. Science teachers
themselves see it as a problem that so many school pupils find school science an

unsatisfying experience, though over the last few years more and more pupils, including girls, have opted for science subjects.

In spite of excellent documentaries, and some good popular science magazines, scientific stories in the media still usually alternate between miracle and scientific threat. The popular stereotype of science is like the magic of fairy tales: it has potential for enormous good or awful harm. Popular fiction is full of "good" scientists saving the world, and "mad" scientists trying to destroy it.

From all the many scientific stories which might be given media treatment, those which are chosen are usually those which can be framed in terms of the usual news angles: novelty, threat, conflict or the bizarre. The routine and often tedious work of the scientist slips from view, to be replaced with a picture of scientists forever offending public moral sensibilities (as in embryo research), threatening public health (as in weapons research), or fighting it out with each other (in giving evidence at public enquiries such as those held on the issues connected with nuclear power).

The mass media also tend to over-personalise scientific work, depicting it as the product of individual genius, while neglecting the social organisation which makes scientific work possible. A further effect of this is that science comes to be seen as a thing in itself: a kind of unpredictable force; a tide of scientific progress.

It is no such thing, of course. Science is what scientists do; what they do is what a particular kind of society facilitates, and what is done with their work depends very much on who has the power to turn their discoveries into technology, and what their interests are.

36 According to the passage, ordinary people have a poor opinion of science
    and scientists because
    A opinion polls are unflattering.
    B science is badly taught in schools.
    C scientists are shown negatively in the media.
    D science is considered to be dangerous.

37 Fewer girls than boys study science because
    A they think that science is too difficult.
    B science is seen as a man's job.
    C they are often unsuccessful in science at school.
    D science teachers do not encourage girls.

38 Media treatment of science tends to concentrate on
    A the routine, everyday work of scientists.
    B discoveries that the public will understand.
    C the satisfactions of scientific work.
    D the more sensational aspects of science.

39 According to the author, scientific work is stimulated by
   A   ambition.
   B   social demands.
   C   technological problems.
   D   internal pressures.

40 The author believes that the popular view of science is
   A   accurate.
   B   well-informed.
   C   biased.
   D   over-optimistic.

PAPER 2   COMPOSITION   (2 hours)

*Write **two only** of the following composition exercises. Your answers must follow exactly the instructions given. Write in pen, not pencil. You are allowed to make alterations, but see that your work is clear and easy to read.*

1   Write about the pleasure you get from hobbies and pastimes. (About 350 words)

2   "What you learn outside the classroom is of more importance than what you learn inside it." Discuss. (About 350 words)

3   Write a story that ends as follows: "She took one final look, then carefully closed the door behind her." (About 350 words)

4   A busy self-service restaurant has recently received a number of complaints, some of which are printed below. As manager, write a report to your employer explaining how these complaints came to be made and what should be done to improve the situation. (About 300 words)

- **I can never find a tray!**

- *The queues are so long that my food was cold by the time I found a table.*

- Nobody takes any notice of the NO SMOKING signs.

- *I had to wait more than ten minutes for clean cutlery and a clean glass.*

- **My little boy slipped on the greasy floor.**

5   Basing your answer on your reading of the prescribed text concerned, answer **one** of the following. (About 350 words)

GRAHAM GREENE: *The Quiet American*
How do events of the war develop our understanding of Pyle?

JANE AUSTEN: *Persuasion*
Explain how Captain Wentworth's feelings for Anne Elliot change, and describe the incidents which lead to their engagement.

ANITA BROOKNER: *Hotel du Lac*
What part does Mr Neville play in the novel and is Edith wise in the end not to marry him?

PAPER 3   USE OF ENGLISH   (2 hours)

SECTION A

1   *Fill each of the numbered blanks in the following pasage with* **one** *suitable word.*

Because we feel tired at bed-time it is natural to assume that we sleep because we are tired. The point seems so obvious that .... (1) anyone has ever sought to question .... (2). Nevertheless we must ask "tired .... (3) what?" People certainly feel tired at the end of a hard day's manual work, but it is also .... (4) that office workers feel equally tired when bed-time comes. Even invalids, ... (5) to beds or wheelchairs, become tired as the evening wears .... (6). Moreover, the manual worker .... (7) still feel tired even .... (8) an evening spent relaxing in front of the television or .... (9) a book, activities which .... (10) to have a refreshing .... (11). There is .... (12) proven connection between physical exertion and the .... (13) for sleep. People want to sleep, ... (14) little exercise they have had. .... (15) is the desire for sleep related to mental fatigue. In fact, sleep comes more slowly .... (16) people who have had an intellectually stimulating day, ... (17) because their minds are still full of thoughts .... (18) they retire. Ironically, one way of sending .... (19) to sleep is to put him or her into a boring situation .... (20) the intellectual effort is minimal.

2   *Finish each of the following sentences in such a way that it is as similar as possible in meaning to the sentence printed before it.*

EXAMPLE: I expect that he will get there by lunchtime.

ANSWER: I expect him *to get there by lunchtime.*

75

a) Our hotel booking hasn't been confirmed.

    We haven't received ....

b) The salesman told me that my new car would be delivered next Wednesday.

    According ....

c) The Yeti has very rarely been seen at this altitude.

    There have ....

d) It is not certain that Jones will get the job.

    It is open ....

e) Everyone started complaining the moment the announcement was made.

    No sooner ....

f) As I get older, I want to travel less.

    The older ....

g) A house in that district will cost you at least £100,000.

    You won't be able ....

h) Alan worked too hard at the office, and this led to his illness.

    Alan's illness ....

3 *Fill each of the blanks with a suitable word or phrase.*

    EXAMPLE: He doesn't mind one way or the other; it makes *no difference to* him.

a) She is not used .... her authority questioned.

b) I don't know .... to pass your music exam when you haven't done any practice.

c) I wish .... earlier because then I could have arranged to meet you at the station.

d) While the teacher's back .... , Jimmy passed a note across the classroom.

e) I don't want .... be any disagreement later, so I've written a summary of our discussion.

f) I'm sorry to .... waiting: I've been sitting in a traffic jam for the last two hours.

4   *For each of the sentences below, write a new sentence* **as similar as possible in meaning to the original sentence,** *but using the word given. This word* **must not be altered** *in any way.*

EXAMPLE: Not many people attended the meeting.
turnout

ANSWER: *There was a poor turnout for the meeting.*

a) Mr Watson managed to repair the garage roof only because his neighbour helped him.
without

....

b) Nobody is infallible.
mistakes

....

c) The last Olympic Games were held in Seoul.
took

....

d) He talked about nothing except the weather.
sole

....

e) In the end, I felt I had been right to leave the club.
regrets

....

f) It is stupid of you to refuse Richard's offer of a loan.
   idiot

   ....

g) The company has decided to replace this model.
   intention

   ....

h) In the next few years we'll probably hear a lot more about
   environmental pollution.
   likely

   ....

SECTION B

5 *Read the following passage, then answer the questions which follow it.*

Commuting by motorcycle

If a fast-talking salesman got you in a corner and told you that, with an
outlay of around £2 a week, you could save £57,500 in the next twenty
years, you would be forgiven for calling the police. Now, please don't
call them, because I've saved just that.

It's very simple. Instead of taking the car to work each day, buy a   5
motorcycle and ride it instead. After you get over the initial and
appalling fright, you will find that there is hardly any more danger than
dropping a lit cigar down the inside of your car coat, and that you are,
most of the time, the only vehicle able to move.

I've just completed twenty years of motorcycling from home to work –   10
about ten miles a day on average. The £57,000 is the difference in cost –
purchases, licences, petrol, parking, insurance and servicing – between
the average bike and car. Mind you, I haven't got the £57,000 to actually
show you, but it must be around somewhere.

There's another bit of interesting arithmetic; since my trip into town   15
takes about fifteen minutes on the bike, and is often over an hour in the
car, it means that during the twenty years I've saved the equivalent of
three working years. Does this mean that I owe the government three
years' income tax? I wonder where that extra income is? Or did I have a
three-year holiday without realising it?   20

Come to think of it, the three years may have been the period I spent
fighting the new helmet law. Of course I saw the sense in it, but I hated
being dictated to about what I put on my head, so I wore a British army
paratroop hat. It looked pretty silly, especially since, at the time, I was

riding something called a Monkey Bike (and actually made for circus 25
monkeys), but I did feel foolishly independent. I must have wasted
thousands of hours of police time; riveting arguments ensued until I
managed to get a letter from a commissioner at Scotland Yard allowing
that the hat did fall within the law. Perhaps I should rephrase that.

I wish I still had the Monkey Bike. It was so small that I could put it 30
under my desk at work, and so narrow that I managed once to get away
from a motorcycle policeman by squeezing at full throttle between two
stationary buses on the Kings Road. He didn't fit; I got clean away. It did
have one distinct disadvantage, however – it was so low that when I
pulled up once beside a taxi to wait for a light to change, the driver 35
didn't see me, suddenly opened his window, and covered me with
peanut shells. On reflection he probably did see me and simply knew his
bikes. I even took the bike on the plane to Paris, calling it hand luggage.

All bikers will confirm that the feeling of freedom and independence
is the most important factor in continuing to travel on two wheels. 40
Breathing traffic fumes for 15 minutes must be healthier than breathing
them while stuck in a traffic jam for two hours. And the independence
has become easier in recent years. When bikes were a relative rarity on
London streets, there was a lot of hate and jealousy in the minds of
motorists. Most of us were attacked by cars and taxis. 45

In spite of the horrendous increase in car traffic, I can still plan, with
great accuracy, how long it will take to get from my studio near the Post
Office Tower to a meeting in the City (nine minutes if all the lights are
green). Colleagues are amazed that I continue to turn up on my bike come
rain or shine, but I tell them you can get just as wet trying to hail a taxi!

a) What is so extraordinary about the salesman's proposal in the first
    paragraph?

    ....

b) What was the writer's original reaction to the idea of riding a motor-
    cycle?

    ....

    ....

c) What circumstances have helped to form the writer's present opinion of
    commuting by motorcycle?

    ....

    ....

d) What does the figure of £57,000 represent to the writer?

....

....

e) Why does the writer consider the arithmetic in paragraphs 3 and 4 to be "interesting"?

....

f) How did the writer show his dislike of "the new helmet law" (line 22)?

....

g) Why did the writer feel "foolishly independent" (line 26)?

....

....

h) What was it that "wasted thousands of hours of police time" according to the writer (lines 26–27)?

....

....

i) What does the phrase "the hat did fall within the law" mean (line 29)?

....

j) In what three ways did the size of the Monkey Bike benefit the writer?

....

....

....

k) Give two reasons why motorists might feel jealous of bikers according to the writer.

....

....

l) Why doesn't the writer consider the British weather a disadvantage to motorcyclists?

....

m) In a paragraph of 70–90 words explain why the writer feels commuting by motorcycle in London is preferable to using a car.

....

....

....

....

....

....

....

....

....

....

....

....

....

PAPER 4   LISTENING COMPREHENSION
(about 30 minutes)

PART ONE

You will hear a local radio news bulletin. For each of the questions 1–10, tick one box to show whether the statement is true or false.

	True	False
1 The Shell company is being allowed to drill for oil at Denny Lodge.		
2 Charles Pasco is not very worried by the oil search.		
3 He thinks they will probably find oil there.		
4 The pool was closed after an accident to a club member.		
5 The damage was caused by men working on the roof.		
6 The announcer has often been to Blandford Forum Camera Club quiz evenings.		
7 The weather at Rotherham has worsened.		
8 The football match has been put off till tomorrow.		
9 Mark Sibley will be available for advice once a week.		
10 His organisation has already been advising people in the area.		

PART TWO

*You will hear a news report of a kidnapping. For questions 11–19, complete the summary of the news report below, by writing **one word** in each box provided.*

BRISTOL ATTACK

A Bristol man was sent to jail for four years today as a result of an attack on ...(11).... Richard Farmer was appearing in ...(12)... on a charge of ...(13)... when he started to attack Lucy Clarke with a carafe he had ...(14).... Farmer did not ...(15)... Mrs Clarke but the police officer who restrained him suffered ...(16)... on his hands and ...(17).... Mrs Clarke remained ...(18)... throughout her ordeal and was subsequently ...(19)... by the judge.

11	
12	
13	
14	
15	
16	
17	
18	
19	

PART THREE

You will hear a woman talking about her job with an organisation called Portage. For each of the questions 20–23, tick one of the boxes A, B, C or D to show the correct answer.

20   The Portage Scheme is designed to

    A   provide training for very young handicapped children.

    B   provide a challenge for bright pre-school children.

    C   help children who have fallen behind at school.

    D   help children who are too ill to go to school.

A	
B	
C	
D	

21   What is the first visit used for?

    A   to start teaching

    B   to assess the child

    C   to explain the scheme

    D   to write the activity chart

A	
B	
C	
D	

22 The activity chart is

    A   monitored by the parents.

    B   written by supervisors.

    C   written specially for the individual.

    D   designed by the parents.

A	
B	
C	
D	

23 Why do parents prefer the Portage Scheme to hospital visits?

    A   It is more convenient.

    B   The child is more talkative.

    C   The child is more relaxed.

    D   The attention is better.

A	
B	
C	
D	

PAPER 5   INTERVIEW   (15–20 minutes)

You will be asked to take part in a conversation with a group of other students or with your teacher. The conversation will be based on one particular topic area or theme, for example holidays, work, food.

Of course each interview will be different for each student or group of students, but a *typical* interview is described below.

★ At the start of the interview you will be asked to talk about one of the photographs among the Interview Exercises at the back of the book.

★ You will then be asked to discuss one of the passages at the back of the book. Your teacher may ask you to talk about its content, where you think it comes from, who the author or speaker is, whether you agree or disagree with it, and so on. You will *not* be asked to read the passage aloud, but you may quote parts of it to make your point.

★ You may then be asked to discuss for example an advertisement, a leaflet, extract from a newspaper etc. Your teacher will tell you which of the Interview Exercises to look at.

★ You may also be asked to take part in an activity with a group of other students or your teacher. Your teacher will tell you which section among the Interview Exercises you should look at.

Practice Test 5

PAPER 1   READING COMPREHENSION   (1 hour)

Answer all questions. Indicate your choice of answer in every case **on the separate answer sheet** *already given out, which should show your name and examination index number. Follow carefully the instructions about how to record your answers. Give* **one answer only** *to each question. Marks will not be deducted for wrong answers: your total score on this test will be the number of correct answers you give.*

SECTION A

In this section you must choose the word or phrase which best completes each sentence. **On your answer sheet** *indicate the letter A, B, C or D against the number of each item 1 to 25 for the word or phrase you choose.*

1   The woman was .... from hospital yesterday only a week after her operation.
   A ejected   B expelled   C evicted   D discharged

2   .... further rioting to occur, the government would be forced to use its emergency powers.
   A Should   B Did   C Were   D Had

3   Unfortunately our local cinema is on the .... of closing down.
   A verge   B hint   C edge   D threat

4   All courses at the college are offered on a full-time basis unless ....
   indicated.
   A further   B otherwise   C below   D differently

5   Your argument .... that Britain is still a great power, but this is no longer the case.
   A outlines   B presupposes   C concerns   D presents

6   The construction of the new road is .... winning the support of local residents.
   A thanks to   B reliant on   C dependent on   D responsible to

7   Although he didn't actually say he wanted a radio for his birthday he did .... pretty strongly.
   A imply   B suggest   C mention   D hint

8 Because of cutbacks in council spending, plans for the new swimming pool had to be ....
   A stockpiled   B overthrown   C shelved   D disrupted

9 Don't let that old rascal take you .... with his clever talk – none of it's true.
   A along   B in   C about   D down

10 People living abroad are not .... to enter for this competition.
   A enabled   B permissible   C capable   D eligible

11 David is captain of the school basketball team, ... his father before him.
   A similar to   B just like   C such as   D as well as

12 The scheme is too expensive to be .... at the present moment.
   A compatible   B liable   C feasible   D accessible

13 He was very upset when the boss passed him .... and promoted a newcomer to the assistant's job.
   A by   B up   C over   D aside

14 Six novels a year, you say? He's certainly a .... writer.
   A fruitful   B fertile   C virile   D prolific

15 The case against the bank robbers was .... for lack of evidence.
   A discarded   B dismissed   C refused   D eliminated

16 Please .... from smoking until the plane is airborne.
   A refrain   B exclude   C resist   D restrain

17 We're planning a holiday in Hong Kong when Peter retires but I don't know whether it'll really ever come ....
   A on   B out   C off   D round

18 No matter how angry he was, he would never .... to violence.
   A resolve   B recourse   C exert   D resort

19 The best soil was .... away by a torrential rainstorm.
   A gushed   B flowed   C flooded   D washed

20 Five readers .... the correct solution to our recent competition.
   A communicated   B qualified   C submitted   D subscribed

21 I'll go on a diet if you ....
   A would   B should   C will   D shall

22 They are happily married although, of course, they argue ....
   A most times   B from day to day   C every now and then   D on
   the occasion

23 During the evening football match the stadium was illuminated by
   ....
   A spotlights   B flashlights   C highlights   D floodlights

24 The 10% discount is only applicable .... items costing over £100.
   A for   B to   C against   D on

25 Owing to the fog, his flight from Karachi was ....
   A belated   B overdue   C unscheduled   D unpunctual

SECTION B

*In this section you will find after each of the passages a number of questions or
unfinished statements about the passage, each with four suggested answers or ways of
finishing. You must choose the one which you think fits best according to the passage.*
On your answer sheet, *indicate the letter A, B, C or D against the number of each
item 26 to 40 for the answer you choose. Give* **one answer only** *to each question.
Read each passage right through before choosing your answers.*

FIRST PASSAGE

Mr Handforth in his old age, in his second childhood – advanced by his
stroke – had kept his wits about him, and they, as old people's wits
sometimes will, inclined him to be critical of those who were nearest and
dearest to him.

Undoubtedly, it was Judith who was – or who had been – nearest and   5
dearest to him. Throughout the many years of his widowerhood – how
many! – she had been at his beck and call, neglecting, as she herself had
said and as he had had ample opportunities of confirming, her own family
and her own affairs to console him in his solitude. She had even suggested,
and he had gratefully though guiltily agreed to her suggestion, that her   10
family would have been larger than it was, that Charlotte might have had
brothers and sisters, as Seymour hoped she would have, if she had not felt
that her father was her first priority.

This combined feeling of guilt and gratitude he had tried to acknowledge
to her from time to time, by presents smaller and greater; and he had made   15
and re-made his will many times, with the object of leaving the residue of
his estate, already much reduced by Judith's inroads on it, in unequal
shares, to Judith and Hester – shares that should seem equal, though they
were not. Thus he got his house and its contents valued at a very low figure,

well knowing that it would be worth far more at his death, to balance a   20
rather high figure of shares to Hester, the value of which he had good
reason for thinking would go down rather than up.

Not that he was not fond of Hester, but in his mind and affections she
had always played second fiddle to her sister; though younger, she had
married earlier; like an almost unfledged bird she had abandoned the nest,   25
and made another for herself far, far away. It was natural, of course; Jack
had swept her off her feet, she had thrown in her lot with him, leaving her
father to Judith's very tender mercies.

How can one feel towards someone who, for the most natural reasons in
the world, has thrown one over as one feels towards someone who, for the   30
best reasons in the world, has stayed by one's side?

But were they the best reasons in the world? No, Mr Handforth decided,
they were the worst; everything his daughter Judith had done for him, all
her kindness and her assiduous attentions when he had been alone and/or
ill, had been inspired by one motive, and only one: the greed of gain. At last   35
she had shown herself in her true colours – the colours, whatever they were,
of a vampire.

26 In paragraph 2 the author implies that Judith helped her father
    A   without expecting any gratitude.
    B   while ensuring that he recognised her sacrifice.
    C   because she felt her family came first.
    D   simply out of daughterly affection.

27 Which phrase describes Judith's character in an ironic way?
    A   "Judith's very tender mercies" (line 28)
    B   "her kindness and her assiduous attentions" (line 34)
    C   "the greed of gain" (line 35)
    D   "her true colours" (line 36)

28 In his will Mr Handforth intended to
    A   reward Judith for her sacrifices.
    B   be fair to both sisters.
    C   show Judith he had noticed her greed.
    D   give Judith less than Hester.

29 He considered that Hester
    A   had treated him badly.
    B   did not feel anything for him.
    C   had acted reasonably.
    D   had got what she deserved.

30 His sceptical view of Judith
    A   had always been kept secret.
    B   had come about suddenly.
    C   continued to shock him.
    D   was encouraged by Hester.

SECOND PASSAGE

Writers learn as apprentices do except that they have no master to work for
except themselves and the market.

The fact is that writing is an empirical art, which can only be learned by doing
it. This fact is no reflection on the art of writing. Because skill is acquired in a
seemingly haphazard way, it is none the worse, indeed sometimes the better,
for it. As in every art you must have at least the foundation of a gift, without
which it is useless to proceed; but if the foundation exists, then success – not
merely economic – is largely a matter of persistence and of making the most of
opportunities. Experience is a hard school. Wastage among aspiring writers is
high and most survivors have to rely on another job. The pros and cons of that
situation are debatable. Working out in the world is not solely a form of
insurance; it can also be a vital source of material and incentive, particularly for
the fiction writer. Many well-known authors laboured away at other jobs for
part or all of their lives, and either profited therefrom or made their names
notwithstanding.

Economic security frees the mind from worry, but a routine job also
consumes mental energy which might otherwise be harnessed to creative
output. This applies as much to freelance journalism and other ancillary
activities of authorship as to non-literary employment. A regular stint of
reviewing, reading manuscripts for publishers, broadcasting, lecturing, and the
like, may oil the machinery of the mind, but it may also use up horsepower to
the point of exhaustion. Moreover, continuity of creation is often vital –
whether for the construction of a work of fiction or for historical research or,
indeed, for any idea that has to be digested into literary form. Interruptions
nowadays, however, are a professional hazard that all authors have to contend
with, but they are not insuperable and not the worst threat to a living literature.

31 According to the author, how is the skill of writing acquired?
    A   by methodical practice
    B   by studying the market
    C   by following another writer's example
    D   by producing one's own work

32 In the author's opinion, it is impossible to become a successful writer
    without
    A   some talent.
    B   early publication.
    C   another source of income.
    D   consideration for the reader.

33 How does the author regard a writer's second job?
    A   usually harmful to one's writing
    B   essential in most cases
    C   too time-consuming
    D   helpful in researching facts

34 How might a second job damage a writer?
    A   by restricting his imagination
    B   by using up his mental strength
    C   by destroying his talent
    D   by removing the need to write

35 How do modern writers differ from those of the past?
    A   They have less mental energy.
    B   They need to rely on another job.
    C   They cannot expect to work without interruption.
    D   They learn their art more thoroughly.

THIRD PASSAGE

In a world increasingly fearsome and fragile, TV commercials represent an oasis
of calm and reassurance. For six minutes in every hour, viewers know that they
will be wafted away from this cruel world into an idealised well-ordered land.
You and I may experience real life as largely harassed and chaotic but in the
world of the TV commercials happy families may be relied upon to gather at
breakfast-time for convivial bowls of cornflakes, their teeth free of decay, their
hair innocent of dandruff, their shirts whiter than snow.

TV advertising in Britain, obsessed with the symbols of the good life, exploits
a yearning for evidence of old-fashioned security. Things were better in the old
days: bread was crusty and beer was a man's drink. But in selling the idea of a
better life, it strikes me that most British commercials fail in their primary
function. I cannot be alone among those who usually remember everything
about TV advertising except the product it is designed to publicise.

In one superb commercial, a distinguished-looking Italian butler drives a car
headlong into a vast dining-hall to serve champagne. What on earth was it
selling? The champagne? The car? What car? Search me. Viewers revelled in the
medium and forgot the message. American advertisers don't make such
mistakes. A typical U.S. commercial features a woman in a kitchen holding a

highly-visible bottle of something or other and selling it hard. No art, no craft, just the message. America sells the steak, while Britain sells the sizzle.

A nation needs symbols. We need proof that lovely things still endure, like a team of shire horses criss-crossing the landscape at sundown. We want to be reminded that they still exist, that we may still come across pockets of sanity and beauty in a world less sane and less beautiful each day. TV commercials provide us with those symbols. They provide a link with the way we like to think we were. They help us to keep in touch with lost innocence.

36 Families in TV commercials are usually depicted as
    A   self-indulgent.
    B   wealthy.
    C   idealistic.
    D   carefree.

37 British TV advertising concentrates on
    A   the appearance of the product.
    B   the emotional needs of its audience.
    C   the quality of modern life.
    D   the need for good quality products.

38 What does the writer think of the car commercial?
    A   It was too long.
    B   It did not achieve its main aim.
    C   It lacked originality.
    D   It was poorly produced.

39 How are British commercials different from American ones?
    A   They adopt a more subtle approach.
    B   They are generally of a lower standard.
    C   They are more expensively produced.
    D   They communicate more effectively.

40 In the last paragraph, the writer suggests that British TV advertising
    A   accurately reflects modern life.
    B   is too old-fashioned.
    C   fulfils a useful function.
    D   concentrates on unimportant things.

PAPER 2 COMPOSITION (2 hours)

*Write **two only** of the following composition exercises. Your answers must follow exactly the instructions given. Write in pen, not pencil. You are allowed to make alterations, but make sure that your work is clear and easy to read.*

1 Describe what people in your country like to do on their day off. (About 350 words)

2 Today man is damaging and may be destroying his environment. What measures do you think should be taken to prevent this happening? (About 350 words)

3 Write a short story ending with the words: "He stood on the bridge tearing the paper into tiny pieces and dropping the scraps into the water. Then he turned and walked away; it was over." (About 350 words)

4 A new hospital has opened in your town. You are a reporter for your local newspaper and your editor has asked you to write an article about people's reactions to the new hospital. Noted below are some comments from local people; use these to help you write the article. (About 300 words)

- Brand-new technology and small wards
- Will cater for everyone in the community
- Offers a variety of new jobs in the area
- Emergency/casualty unit will save lives
- Cuts down on queues to see doctors
- No more long journeys to Central Hospital

>>>→

5   Basing your answer on your reading of the prescribed text concerned, answer **one** of the following. (About 350 words)

GRAHAM GREENE: *The Quiet American*
"He was a very quiet American." Does the description help us to understand who Pyle is and what he does?

JANE AUSTEN: *Persuasion*
Describe Anne and Elizabeth Elliot. How far does the interest of the novel arise from their different characters?

ANITA BROOKNER: *Hotel du Lac*
The telegram Edith wrote at the end of the book contained only one word: "Returning." Is this the ending the reader expects?

PAPER 3   USE OF ENGLISH   (2 hours)

SECTION A

1   *Fill each of the numbered blanks in the following passage with* **one** *suitable word.*

We are living at a critical point in our history. Once ....(1) a time primitive peoples feared storms and the night, and lived by superstitions. Then science rationalised things and created order, and brought us to the point ....(2) we could invent theories of creation and ....(3) them in the laboratory. We began to feel omnipotent. We were aware that ....(4) were man-made threats which could wipe us off the ....(5) of the Earth. But the Universe would go on for ....(6).

Now we are not ....(7) sure. We are becoming increasingly ....(8) of our vulnerability, and so far have done very ....(9) about it. With planning we ....(10), one day, escape the Earth and colonise space. After ....(11), transatlantic flight is commonplace today but would have been ....(12) a dream in Columbus' time, five hundred years ago.

More than a ....(13) scientists believe that mankind's arrival is so improbable that it is as if Nature conspired to bring it ....(14). They see hints that the Universe created life to be its agents for immortality. As ....(15) as we know, we are the ones who have to carry out the task. ....(16) we can avoid extinction in the short ....(17), then we may propagate throughout space into the indefinite future. You and I have no ....(18) to life; we inherited it by ....(19). Now that we are here, we have the duty to ....(20) our part in the great human relay race.

2 *Finish each of the following sentences in such a way that it is as similar as possible in meaning to the sentence printed before it.*

   EXAMPLE: I expect that he will get there by lunchtime.

   ANSWER: I expect him *to get there by lunchtime.*

a) Keeping calm is the secret of passing your driving test.

   As long as ....

b) Immediately after his appointment to the post, the new editor fell ill.

   No sooner ....

c) The protest has been so vociferous that the committee has had to reconsider.

   There has been ....

d) You think that fat people are always jolly, but you are wrong.

   Contrary ....

e) My boss works better when he's pressed for time.

   The less ....

f) The patient recovered more rapidly than expected.

   The patient made ....

g) There isn't a pair of thermal socks left in the shop, madam!

   We are completely ....

h) Their chances of success are small.

   It is not ....

3 *Fill each of the blanks with a suitable word or phrase.*

   EXAMPLE: He doesn't mind one way or the other; it makes *no difference to* him.

a) All the best seats .... if we don't get to the meeting on time.

b) Everything that .... go wrong did go wrong!

c) Twelve votes were cast .... of the resolution and only three against.

d) They were talking so loudly that she .... overhearing what they said.

e) If only .... your offer of help! I found organising the party on my own very difficult.

f) You'd be better off buying a new washing machine .... your old one repaired.

4 *For each of the sentences below, write a new sentence* **as similar as possible in meaning to the original sentence,** *but using the word given. This word* **must not be altered** *in any way.*

EXAMPLE: Not many people attended the meeting.
   turnout

ANSWER: *There was a poor turnout for the meeting.*

a) Their problems are all self-inflicted.
   making

   ....

b) The travel agent was able to offer a 50% reduction on holidays to the Costa Brava.
   half

   ....

c) If you take that job, you'll have to get up at 6 a.m. every morning.
   mean

   ....

d) The only thing they could do was to look for a new flat.
   alternative

   ....

e) His last letter to me was written three years ago.
   heard

   ....

f) If only one could rely on what she says.
   pity

   ....

g) An open fire can't be compared to central heating.
   comparison

   ....

h) I remember very few things about my childhood.
   scarcely

   ....

SECTION B

5 *Read the following passage, then answer the questions which follow it.*

The lost people of Alaska

In March 1985, a young man walked out onto the tundra behind the
small Yukon River Village of Alakkunuk and shot himself through the
heart. The sound of the shot rang out across the flat delta landscape,
punching a hole in the dinner-time darkness of a cold spring day. His
self-destruction marked the beginning of a sixteen-month-long suicide   5
epidemic in which, in a community of just 550 people, eight committed
suicide and a high number of attempted suicides occurred. But while
this may have been the beginning of the problem for this small, remote
village, it is just another statistic in the alarming number of untimely
deaths among native Alaskans over the past few years.   10

Alcohol and drug abuse account for most deaths, but they may not be
the disease. Rather, they seem to be the anaesthetic that numbs a deeper
trouble. When one's culture is invaded by outsiders, it creates despair,
which has been proved time and again in other native societies. The
continual assault of western diseases, western institutions and western 15
economics is destroying the basic life-styles of the native Alaskans.

The invading western traders took advantage of a primitive, bartering
economy and were followed by the missionaries who forcibly removed
the supporting foundations of spirituality. Smallpox and tuberculosis
ravaged the adult population, an exploited generation who are today's   20
grandparents. Then the government took their children away, sending
them to boarding schools hundreds of miles from their villages. They
returned with heightened aspirations, limited prospects and no experience of family life. They turned away from their elders to alcohol.
Today's parents became a lost generation. The village economy became   25
desperate for cash when the natives needed electricity, snow-mobiles –

and alcohol. Improved communications and television have created an appetite among the young, who are between two opposed cultures. Children go to school to learn things that their parents don't know in a language their grandparents don't understand. When they try for higher 30 education, native children, being naturally non-competitive, stand little chance against westerners. Frustrated, they turn to alcohol and have become a generation in danger.

Hunting, fishing and gathering were once the industry, economy and religion of these people. Alcohol and the welfare state have combined to 35 form a vicious circle that the natives cannot escape. The men have been devalued in the eyes of their families. Mothers with children get welfare and food stamps. The old people get security cheques. The women qualify for western-style jobs as secretaries and clerks, while the men find it hard to keep any jobs they get. If a man cannot have time off to 40 fish and hunt for his family, he would rather be unemployed. With the loss of their cultural anchor, many natives have chosen to opt out. Suicide is quick with a bullet, slow from a whisky bottle. In the lingering misery of a disconnected life on the edge of existence, drinking fills the day.

Insufficient record-keeping and a sense of shame among the natives 45 have led to a huge under-recording of native suicides, and village elders deny the existence of alcoholism. In the crisp early morning air, Alakkunuk is quiet except for the occasional footstep on newly fallen snow. As the streets gradually come to life, early risers smile in greeting; trouble is hidden away. But sorrow lines the faces of grandparents, fear 50 clouds the eyes of neglected children, alcohol unsteadies the legs of parents. The problems cannot be hidden or denied any more.

a) Which two phrases are used in the first paragraph to indicate the silence being broken?

....

b) Explain the use of the word "epidemic" in this context (line 6).

....

....

c) Why are the deaths described as "untimely" (line 9)?

....

....

≫≫→

d) What is the "disease" (line 12) if it is not "alcohol and drug abuse"?

....

e) What does the word "diseases" refer to in line 15?

....

....

f) What are the two cultures referred to in line 28?

....

g) Mention two characteristics of each of the "two opposed cultures" (line 28).

....

....

h) How do alcohol and the welfare state create a "vicious circle" (line 36)?

....

....

....

i) How has the men's role in Alaskan society been diminished?

....

....

....

j) Explain what is meant in this context by "cultural anchor" (line 42).

....

....

k) What action is taken by those who decide to "opt out" (line 42)?

....

....

....

l)   Why is it difficult to assess the extent of the social problems in Alaska?

....

....

....

m) In a paragraph of 70–90 words summarise the ways in which western
     influences have affected three generations of Alaskans.

....

....

....

....

....

....

....

....

....

....

....

....

....

PAPER 4   LISTENING COMPREHENSION
(about 30 minutes)

PART ONE

You will hear a story about a honey seller's journey. For each of the questions 1–4, tick one of the boxes A, B, C or D to show the correct answer.

1   Where was the honey seller's customer waiting?

   A   in the next state south

   B   in the village of Lo-ping

   C   two states north

   D   three states away

A	
B	
C	
D	

2   The owner of the cat threw a hammer because he wanted to

   A   hit the owner of the dog.

   B   chase the dog away from the cat.

   C   stop the cat licking up the honey.

   D   keep the dog away from the honey.

A	
B	
C	
D	

3   Why was the honey seller happy?

   A   Because he had not had to fight.

   B   Because he had achieved what he had planned.

   C   Because Lo-ping had not been destroyed.

   D   Because his cousins were safe.

A	
B	
C	
D	

4   The *real* moral of the story is that

   A   a minor accident can have major consequences.

   B   domestic animals need regular feeding.

   C   human beings are naturally aggressive.

   D   people have no control over the world around them.

A	
B	
C	
D	

PART TWO

You will hear a teacher discussing with a colleague a conversation he has just had. For questions 5–12, complete the form he is filling in as appropriate, with a word or short phrase.

WESTEND MIDDLE SCHOOL

Confidential Welfare Report

Pupil's Name : Michael GREGSON

Class : 1M

Name of parents/guardians : | 5 |

Relationship (if other than natural parent) :

| 6 |

Difficulties encountered :

| 7 |

| 8 |

Reaction of parents/guardians :

| 9 |

Teacher's assessment of cause of problem :

| 10 |

Step(s) to be taken by parents/guardians :

| 11 |

Step(s) to be taken by teacher :

| 12 |

PART THREE

You will hear an accountant called Anne talking to her friend Glyn about the firm she works for. For questions 13–17, tick one of the boxes A, B, C or D to show the correct answer.

13   Why is Anne angry?

    A   Her company has been given poor advice.

    B   Her company has made a bad decision.

    C   Her company has been taken over.

    D   Her company expects too much from her.

A	
B	
C	
D	

14   Anne and Glyn think that £300,000 is

    A   a great deal of money.

    B   not much to pay for a firm.

    C   less than the business was worth.

    D   worth taking a risk with.

A	
B	
C	
D	

15   The firm's main problem is

    A   it does not have enough shops.

    B   there is no demand for their product.

    C   the shops are in the wrong place.

    D   it has not done enough to get business.

A	
B	
C	
D	

16   The problem with the firm's premises is that they

    A   do not belong to the firm.

    B   are in the wrong part of town.

    C   are not suitable.

    D   need expensive repairs.

A	
B	
C	
D	

17   The reason Anne's firm bought the business was

    A   they were advised to do so by their accountants.

    B   they think they can develop it.

    C   starting a new business was too expensive.

    D   that they had been misled about its profitability.

A	
B	
C	
D	

PAPER 5   INTERVIEW   (15–20 minutes)

You will be asked to take part in a conversation with a group of other students or with your teacher. The conversation will be based on one particular topic area or theme, for example holidays, work, food.

Of course each interview will be different for each student or group of students, but a *typical* interview is described below.

* At the start of the interview you will be asked to talk about one of the photographs among the Interview Exercises at the back of the book.

* You will then be asked to discuss one of the passages at the back of the book. Your teacher may ask you to talk about its content, where you think it comes from, who the author or speaker is, whether you agree or disagree with it, and so on. You will *not* be asked to read the passage aloud, but you may quote parts of it to make your point.

* You may then be asked to discuss for example an advertisement, a leaflet, extract from a newspaper etc. Your teacher will tell you which of the Interview Exercises to look at.

* You may also be asked to take part in an activity with a group of other students or your teacher. Your teacher will tell you which section among the Interview Exercises you should look at.

Interview Exercises

PRACTICE TEST 1

ADDICTIONS

1

2

3

4 Parents who smoke risk raising sickly children who make "slower progress in reading, writing and other learning," claims a report from the Association for Non-smokers' Rights.
Children in smokers' homes were "more prone to asthma and bronchitis, and could suffer meningitis and lung cancer in later life," said the report's author, Miss Anne Charlton, director of a cancer study group at Manchester University.

5 Patrons are recommended to read the sign at each entrance-way urging players to chance only what they can spare at the gaming tables. Players are not obliged to tip croupiers and any request for a tip by a casino employee may be ignored.

6 Popping in for a pint or two at the local is still the most popular leisure activity, second only to watching TV. And it all started long before the Romans arrived.
What is it that makes the British pub so unique? Is it the beer, the food, the games, the people – or what?

7

"It could never happen to me."
You may be asked how realistic you consider this attitude ("It could never happen to me.") to be in relation to various habits which may become obsessions, e.g.

gambling	watching TV
smoking	making money
drinking	becoming powerful/famous
taking drugs	eating too much/too little

8   "If you have a healthy lifestyle you will never have problems with alcohol, drugs, gambling or any other additions." You may be asked to discuss this statement.

PRACTICE TEST 2

THE MEDIA

1

2

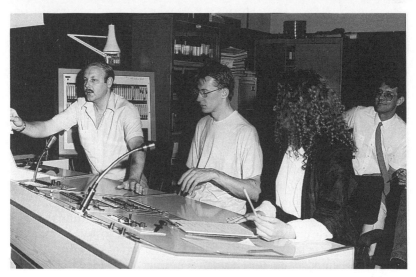

3

4 Philip Jones-Griffiths, whose pictures of suffering civilians in Vietnam formed perhaps the best photographic testament of the war, has said: "Your job is to record for history. You can't feel not involved, but you have to steel yourself and do your job . . . That's what you're there for. It's no use crying. You can't focus with tears in your eyes. It's better to do the breaking down later in the darkroom."

5 Worldwide
News and sport stories are also flashed to the "News" from all over the world, from the Press Association, Reuter and other agencies. Hundreds of items are stored and constantly updated in the computer, and monitored on screen.
In addition, "fax" machines are used to transmit or receive written material instantly.
Reporters can now also plug into the computer – by phone.

6 PICK OF THE DAY

True Stories CANNIBAL TOURS
Dennis O'Rourke's entertaining but shrewdly observed documentary that follows a party of European and American tourists on a luxury cruise deep into the Papua New Guinea jungle. The encounters between the camera-clicking tripper-tribe and the local natives provide some marvellous moments of mutual incomprehension; though it has been screened before, it is a film that

is well worth seeing again for its humour and its underlying message that, while the world gets smaller, cultures do not necessarily shrink to fit.

7 "Good news is no news" (Journalists' catchphrase)

"You don't film certain things on the grounds of taste. You have to be conscious that you are sending pictures into people's living rooms. But I think we do, at times, shelter people too much. News is a serious business. What goes on in the world is not entertainment." (Kate Adie – BBC foreign correspondent)

"The truth is that newspapers want horror but not too much horror. I think if the pictures are too shocking, people quickly turn the page to avoid looking." (Larry Burrows – war photographer)

You may be asked to assess how true these quotations are, and to discuss media coverage of *news* in general and *disasters* in particular.

8 "The picture of the world as painted by the media is far removed from reality."
You may be invited to assess the truth of this statement.

9

New television channel	*New newspaper*
live coverage of the news	news
educational programmes	gossip and scandal
documentary programmes	feature articles
children's programmes	fashion
soap operas	travel and holidays
entertainment	sport
others	foreign news
	crosswords
	horoscopes
	weather
	others

You may be asked to imagine that you are part of a team setting up either a new television channel or a new newspaper. What priority would you give to the topics above and why?

PRACTICE TEST 3

THE SPORTING LIFE

1

2

3

4

Notification of Results

Each team receives stamped addressed match cards before the start of the season. It is the responsibility of the home team to complete and return the score card, countersigned by their opponents *WITHIN ONE WEEK OF A MATCH*. Failure to do so results in the home team being penalised three points.

5

"You can put in your magazine that I have never, ever, in my life taken part in any sport," he quips. "But as an editor and a journalist I've been interested in sport all my life. I'm keen on it; I support Tottenham and if I swam it would not be the length of the baths but the width of my bath."

6

How do I start?

First, think positively. Remember the games you have won against him and not those you have lost.

Second, use the knock-up not as a formality but as the priceless opportunity it really is to get the feel of the ball. Don't try and hit too hard too soon. Get your swing into a groove on both the forehand and backhand.

7

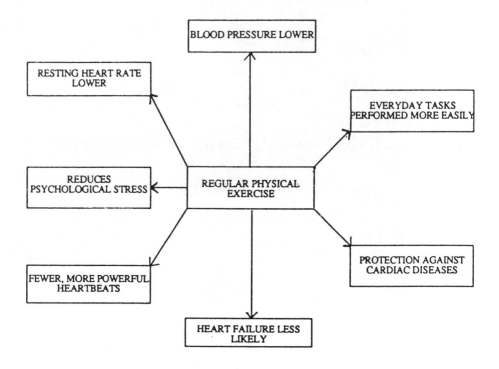

HEALTH AND FITNESS: The benefits of regular physical exercise.

8

You may be asked to discuss the benefits of regular physical exercise.

"In my day, sport belonged to the people – we enjoyed exercise, we enjoyed competition. Now it's all Big Business."

You may be asked for your views on the question above.

PRACTICE TEST 4

LAW AND ORDER

1

2

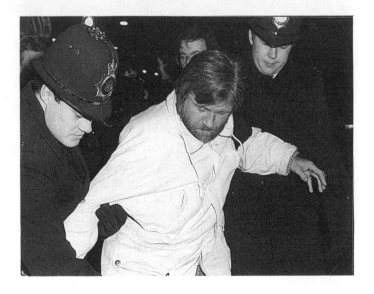

3

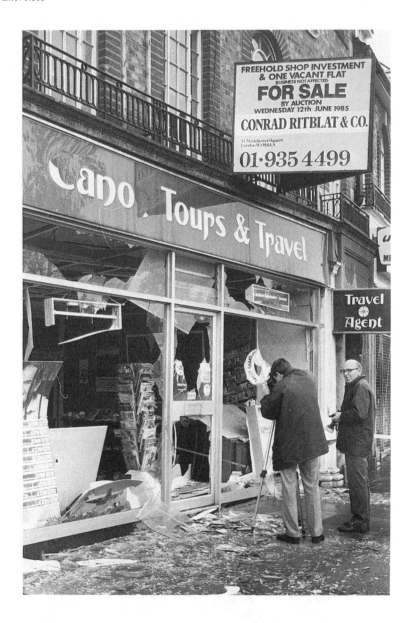

4 It's heartbreaking. This is the third time it's happened to us. No sooner do we get the windows refitted than they're shattered to pieces again. I don't know what the world's coming to, really I don't.

5 The pressures of the job are tremendous. The old role of the friendly bobby on the beat is long gone, I'm afraid. Half the force feel the job's almost impossible nowadays. Times have changed and not for the better.

6 We hold a station Open Day every year and invite the public along to see how we operate. It helps, especially with the younger generation. If we don't make some sort of effort we feel even more isolated as a law-enforcing body.

7 "A short, sharp shock treatment is the only way to deal with young offenders."
You may be asked to discuss the statement above, considering the following possible alternatives:
Open plan prisons
Community care
Probation
Corporal punishment
Compulsory army conscription
Heavy fines
Others

8 *Factors blamed for a rise in violence*
40% Lack of discipline in the home
24% Unemployment
10% Lack of discipline in schools
10% Television
 5% Poor housing/poverty
 4% Break up of old communities
 3% The decline of religion
 3% Don't know
 1% Other

You may be asked to discuss the causes of violence.

PRACTICE TEST 5

WORK AND PLAY

1

2

3

4

Gardening's never looked like this before.
Next introduce their classic lines and colours into the
garden with the new Garden Directory
Browse through over 100 pages at your leisure. It's *Next*
quality at your fingertips. Everything you
need to design and plan the perfect garden from a
beautiful range of over 500 plants, equipment
and accessories. It's full of traditional favourites and
exciting new varieties. With helpful hints on
when, where and how to plant.

5

Leisure Time – we all have it, though sometimes we don't know
quite how to fill it. With this booklet at hand, your worries are over,
for whether you want action, exercise, enjoyment, stimulation or
challenge, it's all here, activity by activity. Cheshire can provide
enough to compare favourably with anywhere else in England. You
will find Cheshire a county of charm; a county for the connoisseur.

6

What's on today
Lancashire: Classically-trained violinist, Tom McConville, at Burnley Mechanics Arts and Entertainments Centre, Manchester Road, Burnley.
Leicestershire: Barnsdale Country Club Young Masters Chess Congress. Tournament begins at 9 a.m. Participants include 22 international masters and four grand masters. Uppingham Community College, London Road, Uppingham, Rutland.

7

You may be asked to discuss the following:
"All work and no play makes Jack a dull boy."
"Pleasure should always give way to business."

8

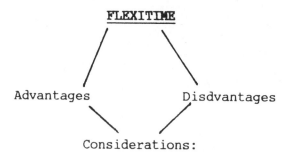

```
            FLEXITIME
           /        \
          /          \
         /            \
   Advantages      Disdvantages
          \          /
           \        /
        Considerations:
```

1. Transport to and from work
2. Home Life
3. Shopping facilities
4. Social life/contact with colleagues
5. Longer hours/shorter week
6. Job satisfaction

You may be asked to imagine that you work in management in a small but growing company. Many employees would like flexible working hours (Flexitime) to be introduced in the company. Discuss the Flexitime chart and decide whether it would be a good thing to introduce Flexitime in your company.

Optional Reading

Jane Austen: *Persuasion*

1

2

3

4 He had been remarkably handsome in his youth; and, at fifty-four, was still a very fine man. Few women could think more of their personal appearance than he did; nor could the valet of any new made lord be more delighted with the place he held in society. He considered the blessing of beauty as inferior only to the blessing of a baronetcy; and the Sir Walter Elliot, who united these gifts, was the constant object of his warmest respect and devotion.

5 Anne Elliot, with all her claims of birth, beauty, and mind, to throw herself away at nineteen; involve herself at nineteen in an engagement with a young man, who had nothing but himself to recommend him, and no hopes of attaining affluence, but in the chances of a most uncertain profession, and no connexions to secure even his farther rise in that profession; would be, indeed, a throwing away, which she grieved to think of!

6 Their house was undoubtedly the best in Camden Place; their drawing-rooms had many decided advantages over all the others which they had either seen or heard of; and the superiority was not less in the style of the fitting-up, or the taste of the furniture. Their acquaintance was exceedingly sought after. Everybody was wanting to visit them. They had drawn back from many introductions, and still were perpetually having cards left by people of whom they knew nothing.

7 Very, very happy were both Elizabeth and Anne Elliot as they walked in. Elizabeth, arm in arm with Miss Carteret, and looking on the broad back of the dowager Viscountess Dalrymple before her, had nothing to wish for which did not seem within her reach; and Anne – but it would be an insult to the nature of Anne's felicity, to draw any comparison between it and her sister's; the origin of one all selfish vanity, of the other all general attachment.

8 There, he had learnt to distinguish between the steadiness of principle and the obstinacy of self-will, between the darings of heedlessness and the resolution of a collected mind. There, he had seen everything to exalt in his estimation the woman he had lost, and there begun to deplore the pride, the folly, the madness of resentment, which had kept him from trying to regain her when thrown in his way.

9   'You should have distinguished', replied Anne. 'You should not have
suspected me now; the case so different, and my age so different. If I
was wrong in yielding to persuasion once, remember that it was to
persuasion exerted on the side of safety, not of risk. When I yielded, I
thought it was to duty; but no duty could be called in aid here. In
marrying a man indifferent to me, all risk would have been incurred,
and all duty violated.'

10   You will be asked to talk about one or more of the following topics.

1   Why Jane Austen called this novel 'Persuasion'
2   What Anne thinks of her father
3   How the three sisters differ from each other
4   Lady Russell's role in the novel
5   Louisa's character
6   Why do you think the Lyme Regis episode is considered to be the
turning point of the novel?
7   What impression do you gain of life in Bath from the novel?

Acknowledgements

The authors and publishers are grateful to the following for permission to reproduce texts and illustrations. It has not been possible to identify sources of all the material used and in such cases the publishers would welcome information from copyright owners.

Rex W. Last for the extract on pp. 4–5 from his book *Language Teaching and the Microcomputer*, published by Basil Blackwell Ltd, 1984; Harper Collins Publishers Limited for the extract on pp. 27–8 from *My Family and Other Animals* by Gerald Durrell; Michael Joseph Ltd for the extract on pp. 48–9 from *Risk* by Dick Francis; the Equal Opportunities Commission for the article entitled *Ageism* by Viki Males from their publication *Equality Now*; Paul Theroux and Hamish Hamilton for the extract on pp. 51–2 from *Sunrise with Seamonsters* by Paul Theroux; New Statesman and Society for the extract on pp. 68–9 from *A Writer Came to our Place* by John Morgan; Hamish Hamilton for the extract on pp. 88–9 from *The Will and the Way* by L.P. Hartley; The Society of Authors for the extract on p. 90 from *Authors by Profession* by Victor Bonham-Carter; New Statesman and Society for the extract on pp. 98–9 from *The Lost People* by Lydia Conway; Paul Popper Ltd for the photographs on pp. 110, 112–13; Advertisers, North London Group for the photographs on pp. 115–16; *Cambridge Evening News* for the photographs on p. 118.

Photographs by John Grant Robertson (p. 106), Nina Hajnal (pp. 107, 109 (top); and T.P. Palomar (p. 119).

Nineteenth-century line drawings on pp. 121–2 by Hugh Thomson.

Book design by Brian Lock.

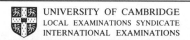
ENTER CANDIDATE NUMBER HERE →

NOW SHOW THE NUMBER BY MARKING THE GRID

Examination/Paper No.

Examination Title

Centre No.

ENTER CANDIDATE NAME HERE:

....

● Tell the Invigilator immediately if the information above is not correct.

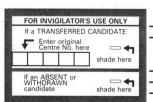

FOR INVIGILATOR'S USE ONLY

If a TRANSFERRED CANDIDATE
Enter original Centre No. here
shade here

If an ABSENT or WITHDRAWN candidate
shade here

M U L T I P L E – C H O I C E   A N S W E R   S H E E T

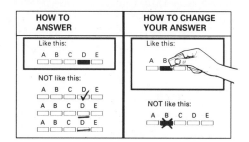

HOW TO ANSWER

Like this:

A B C D E

NOT like this:

A B C D E
A B C D E
A B C D E

HOW TO CHANGE YOUR ANSWER

Like this:

A B

NOT like this:

A B C D E

DO
– use an HB pencil
– rub out any answer you wish to change

DON'T
– use any other kind of pen or pencil
– use correcting fluid
– make any marks outside the boxes

1	A B C D
2	A B C D
3	A B C D
4	A B C D
5	A B C D
6	A B C D
7	A B C D
8	A B C D
9	A B C D
10	A B C D

11	A B C D
12	A B C D
13	A B C D
14	A B C D
15	A B C D
16	A B C D
17	A B C D
18	A B C D
19	A B C D
20	A B C D

21	A B C D
22	A B C D
23	A B C D
24	A B C D
25	A B C D
26	A B C D
27	A B C D
28	A B C D
29	A B C D
30	A B C D

31	A B C D
32	A B C D
33	A B C D
34	A B C D
35	A B C D
36	A B C D
37	A B C D
38	A B C D
39	A B C D
40	A B C D

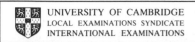

UNIVERSITY OF CAMBRIDGE
LOCAL EXAMINATIONS SYNDICATE
INTERNATIONAL EXAMINATIONS

ENGLISH AS A FOREIGN LANGUAGE

Examination/Paper No.

Examination Title

Centre/Candidate No.

Candidate Name

LISTENING COMPREHENSION ANSWER SHEET

TEST NUMBER		FOR OFFICE USE ONLY	[10] [20] [30] [40] [50] [0] [1] [2] [3] [4] [5] [6] [7] [8] [9]

1	21	41	
2	22	42	
3	23	43	
4	24	44	
5	25	45	
6	26	46	
7	27	47	
8	28	48	
9	29	49	
10	30	50	
11	31	51	
12	32	52	
13	33	53	
14	34	54	
15	35	55	
16	36	56	
17	37	57	
18	38	58	
19	39	59	
20	40	60	

OMR FCE/CPE-4